Wrestle

That

Bear

If there is no struggle, there is no progress.

Those who depreciate [struggles] want crops without plowing the ground.

They want rain without thunder and lightning.

They want the ocean without the roar of the waters.

This struggle may be a moral one; or it may be a physical one; or it may be both. But there must be a struggle before the battle can be won.

—Frederick Douglass,
ex-slave and abolitionist

DEDICATION

To my wife Carol, to my longtime friend Wes Brown, and to my newfound friend Bruce Bouvier for facing their struggles with cancer with grace, courage, and humor.

ACKNOWLEDGMENT

In book publishing, I have the easy job—I write sentences.

The hard work, the creative work, the grunt work, begins after I finish my part, so here's my tribute to the people who make me look good.

Thank you, Jack Parry of Parry Design Studio, for remaining patient while rendering five, six, seven different versions of the cover, only to start from scratch once again when I suggest yet another approach. Your patience is exceeded only by your talent.

Thank you Elizabeth Parry for designing and laying out the text and then painstakingly and patiently making three rounds of edits and corrections to the digitized text you eventually send, with a sigh of relief, to the printer.

Katherine Glover, with whom I've worked for nearly 20 years (where did the time go?), thank you for nurturing the relationships and taking care of the dogged detail work that gets my books from the printer to the buyers.

And thanks to the staff at United Graphics, who have printed millions of my books over the last two decades without missing a single deadline or sending an order to the wrong address.

Thanks, guys. Where would I be without you (don't you dare answer that!)?

Other Books by Dr. Steve W. Price

Household Gold

Dream Making in a Dream-Taking World

WWW. Stands for "World Wide Whiners"

Surviving the Perfect Recession

How to Bounce When Others Break

How to Make Every Day Independence Day

CONTENTS

INTRODUCTION

INTRODUCTION

To Live Is to Struggle

If you can meet triumph and disaster,
And treat those two imposters just the same.

—Rudyard Kipling,
from the poem "If"

Years ago—decades ago, actually—when my brother Mark and I would ask our mom what she wanted for her birthday or Christmas, she'd always give the same three-word answer.

She's spread her arms wide, palms upward, like an ancient priestess imploring the gods, lift her face toward the heavens, and say with a slight smile and an exaggerated sigh, *"Peace of mind. All I ever want is peace of mind."*

Her answer puzzled me at the time. But no longer.

Today, more than 50 years after her pronouncements, I recognize the resounding ring of truth in Mom's answer. I finally understand how much she struggled… how every day was the same as it ever was, a constant struggle to balance a full-time job in a small retail store while raising two rambunctious boys and accommodating my dad, whose drinking, as the years wore on, started earlier in the day and lasted longer into the evening.

About my mom's struggles: She struggled with fatigue... she struggled to manage her time... and she struggled to manage two rowdy boys and a husband slipping deeper and deeper into alcoholism.

Struggled, yes. Complained? No.

My mom, Mary Price, was one of the sunniest, smiling, supportive people I've ever known. For her, struggling wasn't something to dread. Or avoid. Struggling was just something you have to deal with daily, like brushing your teeth before bedtime. Struggles were something you wrestle with and then put an end to and go on to the next struggle. My mom faced her struggles with humor and dignity and determination until she finally succumbed to her final, fatal struggle with cancer at age 72.

To Live Is to Struggle

Growing up poor in rural Indiana during the Great Depression, my mom struggled throughout her childhood... struggled from the day her first cries sifted through the rear screen door of the church parsonage in the tiny coal mining town of Dugger, Indiana, until the day she graduated from high school wearing one of the only two dresses she owned.

The daughter of a Baptist minister struggling to support a wife and four children, my mom's family went from destitute to desperate when the stock market crashed in 1929, ushering in the Great Depression. My mom was only nine when the depression hit, and for the next 11 years, every day of her life was a struggle to survive until she married in 1940 at age 20 and settled into a one-bedroom apartment near Kelly Air Force Base in San Antonio, Texas, with Army Air Corps PFC Ernest Price, who, six years later, became my dad.

Growing up, my mom struggled to get enough to eat. Struggled to find cardboard inserts to cover the holes in the soles of her only pair of shoes. And, as the shyest of four children, struggled for attention from an overworked mother and a strict, distant dad.

For my mom, to live was to struggle. For her, struggling wasn't a rarity to complain about. For her, struggling was a constant, a fact of life, like breathing or doing her daily chores.

'You Gotta Wrestle That Bear'

So, out of necessity, my mom developed a philosophy about how to deal with struggles. Her philosophy boiled down to this: *Like it or not, life is a never-ending series of struggles—most small but some huge—and they're with us every waking moment of every day. So you better get used to dealing with them.*

"You can't run from your problems because they're faster than you and will just chase you down. So, you gotta wrestle that bear," she'd say, raising both arms like she was going to pounce on me. "You gotta face your struggles, stand up to 'em and show 'em who is stronger. Pin 'em on their back, then jump up and get ready to wrestle the next bear, 'cause they travel in packs."

I don't know where her metaphor "wrestle that bear" came from... I just remember hearing her bark the phrase a couple times a week. If I went hitless in a Little League game, she'd encourage me to wrestle that bear by taking more batting practice. Big test tomorrow in biology class? "Turn off the TV and wrestle that bear."

How Struggles Shaped the "Greatest Generation"

I'm proud to say Mom wrestled that bear every day of her 72 years on Earth, and I'm doing my best to live up to her legacy. From my mom I learned that struggles aren't something to avoid, they're something to embrace because they offer us an opportunity to strengthen and define ourselves.

My parents never romanticized their struggles during the Great Depression. Truth is, they were ashamed of growing up poor, as if they caused their struggles by doing something wrong. And they resented what poverty did to them... resented a childhood marked by more pain than pleasure, and, like too many parents of their generation, they compensated for their damaged childhoods by indulging my brother and me with too many things for too little work on our part.

Although my mom shook her head in shame when she told me stories about learning to sit in high school classes with one foot over the other to cover up the missing tongue in her left shoe, she never wanted to erase those memories, which explains her habit of sitting with her right foot on top of her left for the rest of her life. And she never talked about wishing she could swap childhoods with more privileged peers. She owned her history and used it to carve and whittle her future: She was all about putting her family first... she was frugal... she was funny... and she was loyal to a fault, traits that helped her survive a colorless childhood and forge a good and happy life and a 52-year marriage to my dad.

My mom and dad weren't alone in their struggles during the Great Depression. Millions of Americans struggled for survival in the 1930s. But my parents' struggles toughened them and shaped them and other members of "the greatest generation," preparing them to accept with determination and grace and honor the deprivations of the '30s and '40s and to endure the brutal battles of WWII and Korea. And then, beginning in the mid-1940s, with the horror of war behind them, my parents' entire generation, honed and steeled by struggles, turned their energy and optimism to building businesses instead of bombs, creating the most prosperous half century in the history of the world.

What about Millionaires and Billionaires?

Most people assume that money is the magical elixir that can make all their struggles disappear, *poof!*... into thin air. They think that the more money they have, the fewer struggles they'll have.

But just as often the opposite happens—more money only adds its own peculiar side dishes to people's buffet of struggles. Poor people struggle to get their money. Rich people struggle to keep their money. The media is full of stories about lottery winners who burn through millions and end up broker than they were before they hit the jackpot. Or stories about young people who inherit fortunes only to self-destruct on booze and drugs. Or stories about star athletes who burn through tens of millions of dollars in their 20s and 30s and are broke before they reach 40.

For sure, money can mitigate problems in our lives. But it can't eliminate them. Dr. Norman Vincent Peale, the author of the classic bestseller *The Power of Positive Thinking*, loved to tell the story about his rich friend George to illustrate why all of us, rich and poor alike, have to deal with struggles in our lives. The story goes like this:

Walking down the street one day, Dr. Peale ran into his friend George.

"How you doing, George?" asked Dr. Peale brightly.

"Terrible, terrible," moaned George. "All I have is problems. Problems at work. Problems at home. If you could get rid of all my problems, I'd gladly donate $5,000 to your favorite charity."

"Why, George, I'll take you up on that offer," responded Dr. Peale cheerfully. "Recently I was at a place where thousands of people reside, and not a single one has any problems. Would you like meet me there sometime this week?"

"Wow!" shouted George. "I'd love to meet you there. Name the time and place!"

"How about tomorrow at noon?" said Dr. Peale.

"I'll clear my calendar," George said. "Where do we meet?"

"We're meeting at the front gates of Woodlawn Cemetery," replied Dr. Peale with a straight face, "because the only people I know who don't have problems are dead."

The Point and Purpose of This Book

The point of Dr. Peale's story and the point of this book are the same: To live is to struggle. So, since we're all going to face struggles in our lives, we might as well expect and embrace and manage our struggles in ways that will *make us…* instead of allowing our struggles to *break us.*

By its very definition, success means overcoming obstacles to achieve our goals. People who inherit a million dollars or win the lottery are called *lucky,* not successful. But people who confront their struggles… people who use their brains to maneuver around obstacles and their determination to bulldoze through them—those are the people others admire as successful. And those are the people who take pride in their success because they earned it the right way, the old-fashioned way—with brains, hard work, and perseverance.

My purpose in writing this book is to enlighten you about why struggles are not only ennobling but, indeed, *necessary* in our lives, and to remind you not to run from those struggles, but to embrace them… seek them out, even… for without struggles, we can never savor successes. Struggles precede success. The more struggles we have, the more opportunities we have for more success. Winners engage their struggles, wrestle with them, and come out on top.

Faced with the same struggles, losers quit. We're all programmed to respond in one of two ways to struggles: fight or flee. Winners fight. Losers flee. This book is designed to motivate you to fight through your struggles so that you can savor the success after the battle is settled.

What Struggles Are Blocking Your Way to Success?

Let's get real here—you're facing struggles in your life right now and there are more waiting for you in your future.

You may be struggling to pay the bills each month...

You may be struggling with too much credit card debt...

You may be struggling in your job...

You may be struggling with unemployment or, nearly as bad, underemployment...

You may be struggling in your efforts to grow your new business...

You may be struggling to keep the bank from foreclosing on your home...

You may be struggling with your health or illness in your family...

You may be struggling with your weight...

You may be struggling with your kids...

You may be struggling in your marriage...

You may be struggling with depression or anxiety...

You may be struggling with loss of confidence...

You may be struggling to learn a new skill or trade...

You may be struggling with your aging or your aging parents...

Hey, I'm personally acquainted with most of these struggles. Been there, struggled with that, so I've had to wrestle with many of the struggles you're dealing with right now. And, thanks to my mom's words of wisdom, I've come out on the winning end of the wrestling matches more often than not—and so can you.

Look, I know it's tough to understand while you're in the middle of a wrestling match with a burly bear, but struggling is good. If you're struggling, it means you haven't thrown in the towel. If you're struggling, it means you're engaged, you've got your problems in a bear hug, and you're standing upright, holding your own, preventing the bear from putting you on your back.

In fact, take a moment to be thankful for your struggles.

If you're struggling, you're alive.

ROUNDS 1 – 10

ROUND 1

Three Brief Bear Stories...
(and What They Can Teach Us about Our Struggles in Life)

Challenge is a dragon with a gift in its mouth.
...Tame the dragon and the gift is yours.

—Noela Evans

In a book titled *Wrestle That Bear*, you'd expect to hear at least a couple bear stories. Well, I'll do better than that—I've got three for you. All of them are true. And all of them contain a message.

The first story happened just outside Panama City, Florida, in early summer of 2011. John Hearn was in the midst of his daily 12-mile bike ride to work on a two-lane road bounded by deep woods on both sides. He was clipping along at 20 miles an hour when he saw something big and black out of the corner of his eye.

"Then it hit me, and I felt bear all over my leg," Hearn told a reporter for the local newspaper. "I knew it was a bear as soon as I got hit," Hearn continued. "It was like getting tackled in football by a furry, toned, bony body."

Both the bicyclist and the bear were knocked to the ground and shaken up a bit. When their heads cleared, the bear bolted for the woods while Hearn assessed the damage to his body and his bike. Hearn suffered road rash on his elbows, back, and hips, and his neck and back ached for days afterward. The road bike took the brunt of the punishment. The back wheel was ripped off and mangled, and the lightweight frame was bent in two places.

"This is by far the worst damage done to my body and my bike, and I've been hit by three cars in nine years of biking to work," said Hearn. Bear and car collisions are not uncommon in the heavily wooded parts of the Florida Panhandle. The Florida Wildlife Department records an average of 150 incidents of bears colliding with cars or trucks each year, with the vast majority occurring in the Panhandle.

Still, bears running over bicyclists are more rare than double winners of the Florida Lottery. Which is little consolation to John Hearn.

"That bear packed a pretty good punch," said Hearn. "And I'll be on the lookout for them in the future."

Lesson of the Bear and the Bicyclist

I had a similar experience with wildlife in the fall of 2012 as I was driving across Florida from Ft. Myers on the west coast to Jupiter on the opposite coast.

I was about halfway across the state, cruising along a narrow two-lane highway in my car at 65 miles an hour, when I saw a blur headed for my windshield... BAM!—the windshield on the driver's side exploded, spraying shards of glass in my face and lap. There was no shoulder on the crowned asphalt road, so I slowed the car to 30 miles an hour, and, peering between the steering wheel and the dashboard while spitting out tiny pieces of safety glass, I cautiously drove 15 miles to the nearest gas station, where I could assess the damage and call to get my windshield repaired.

A trucker wearing a camouflage baseball hat strode over to the windshield, studied the feathers stuck in the shattered safety glass and said with assurance, "Wild turkey. Happens all the time on this stretch of the road. Likely a young male chasing after a hen. His courtin' days is over now," the trucker said with a low chuckle as he headed back to his rig.

I managed to get a rental car delivered to the glass shop replacing my windshield, and within two hours, I was back on the road to Jupiter. Two days later I dropped the rental car off at the repair shop and completed my return trip to my hometown of Tampa.

Our close encounters with Florida wildlife reminded John Hearn and me of a valuable lesson in life; namely, to *expect the unexpected*. Most of us have periods when life is pretty much trouble free—health is good, money is coming in, kids are happy... then BAM!—something out of the blue, totally unanticipated, smashes into our lives, and we have to pick up the pieces and get our lives back on track.

"It's hard to make predictions, especially about the future," observed syntactically challenged Yogi Berra, Hall of Fame catcher for the New York Yankees. Yep, we know what you mean, Yogi. Just as our lives seem to be under control, our struggles harnessed and tamed, a crisis pops up out of nowhere, and as Yogi would say, "It's déjà vu all over again," and we're obliged to wrestle a bear we never saw coming until it was

3

too late. (We'll talk more about expecting the unexpected in chapter 5, *Black Swans and Berserk Bears.*)

Bears, Like People, Tend to Be Picky

Here's another bear story, and, although this one is a bit comical, it contains a lesson we're all too familiar with.

In the thickly forested Cascade Range north of Tacoma, Washington, state wildlife agents found a bear passed out on the front lawn of Baker Lake Park. The cause was obvious—scattered around the slumbering bear were dozens of empty beer cans. The bear had broken into campers' coolers while they were hiking and used its claws and teeth to puncture the cans.

Then the guzzling began... but not just any cans. This bear was picky.

The beer-loving bear shunned the mass-marketed Busch Lite, sipping only part of one can while guzzling 36 cans of Rainier, a locally brewed beer distributed mostly in the Northwest.

"This is a new one on me," said Fish and Wildlife enforcement Sgt. Bill Heinck. "The bear definitely had a preference. He drank the Rainier and wouldn't drink the Busch." Agents finally chased the groggy bear from the campground, but he returned the next morning. Agents then used a large trap to capture the bear for relocation, baiting the trap with the usual: doughnuts, honey, and, you guessed it, a couple open cans of Rainier. The bear ignored the sweets and went straight for the beer as the cage door clanged shut behind him. Park rangers then transported the bear miles away to a dry part of the park.

So, what can we learn from a boozing bear? Namely this: Like the picky bear, our struggles seem to zero in and target a particular part of our lives: Our finances. Or our health. Or our relationships. Or our business. Yes, the old saw "When it rains it pours" happens from time to time in our lives, but it's been my experience that when struggles rain down on us, they flood one area of our lives while the other areas just get sprinkles.

For example, several years ago I started feeling some stiffness in my right hip after I rode my bike or played tennis. The stiffness got stiffer... then annoyingly painful... then excruciatingly painful... then my limping caused my left ankle to ache... then the pain spread to my neck and shoulders.

My finances were doing fine. My marriage was fine. My kids were fine. My business was fine. But my body was aching like an overworked NFL running back on Monday morning.

Finally, I decided I had wrestled this bear long enough, and in the fall of 2011, I got my right hip replaced. Today the hip feels great. I'm back to playing tennis and biking five days a week. But now the bear is back in our camp, this time zeroing in on my wife's health.

Here's my point: Like that picky bear who shunned one brand of beer while going overboard with another, struggles, it seems, really rain down on one area of our lives at a time... then move to another area later in life... then another area the next month or the next year. "Worry, worry, worry, worry. Sometimes feels like worry is my only friend," says the song. We've all had periods like that in our lives. If you haven't, just hang around long enough and you will.

The Bear and the Bushes

The final story of my bear trilogy has special meaning to me because, well, it happened to me. First, the back story:

In the early 1970s, I spent three summers teaching tennis at The Timbers, a mountainside resort outside Steamboat Springs, Colorado. The Timbers featured three main buildings and eight tennis courts. The 30-acre complex was literally cut into a mountainside, with breathtaking views of the valley below. The walkways and stairs connecting the three main buildings had long stretches of level walkways interrupted by steep stairs to the next landing. Thick brush lined most of the walkways on the mountainside.

Now, among the staff it was well known that I had an exaggerated fear of bears. I'd done some overnight backpacking in the mountains surrounding The Timbers, and on several occasions I was jolted out of my sleeping bag by a snorting bear rummaging through camp looking for food. I'd heard many accounts of backpackers run-ins with bears, some of them fatal, so my fears were well-founded, although, I must admit, they bordered on phobic.

During one late-night dinner at The Timbers, I took a lot of teasing about my bear phobia. My explanation was simple: Bears have big claws; camping tents are made of thin nylon. Ergo, nylon tents and its occupants are to hungry bears what cellophane wrappers and Twinkies are to hungry humans— easy to open and sinfully delicious. At least that was my line of reasoning.

So, post dinner the staff and guests teased me mercilessly about my fear of bears. I laughed right along with them until the restaurant closed down, and we all headed down the dimly lit landing to our sleeping quarters. About halfway to my dorm I heard rustling in the bushes next to the walkway. I froze. The rustling stopped. I took two more steps and heard more rustling accompanied by grunting sounds.

"A BEAR!" my mind screamed to my body, and I streaked down the wooden walkway at warp speed, bounding down the steps until I lunged through the door of my dorm. As I leaned against the door, huffing to catch my breath, I could hear footsteps and peals of laughter growing shriller and louder as they trickled down to my door.

I'd been "punked," to use today's parlance, the victim of a practical joke. What I thought was a bear in the bushes was actually two female staffers who left our dinner table early and had bushwhacked me on my way to my room.

I took a good ribbing for the remainder of the week, and for the rest of the summer, I received Twinkies with notes attached, such as "Bear-ly a day goes by I don't 'Twink' of you! Hungrily Yours, Smokey the Bear."

Borrowing on Worry

My irrational fear of bears and the ensuing jokes at my expense were sophomoric and silly, yes, but there's a serious lesson here: All too often we borrow on worry, meaning *we mentally manufacture struggles that will never occur.*

I mean, why should anyone spend time worrying about struggles that may never occur when we all have enough real struggles that need our immediate attention? But we're all guilty of borrowing on worry, aren't we? Like children, too often our imagination runs amok, and we have panic attacks about the monster under our bed. So, we struggle to find ways to thwart the attack—we leave lights on and doors open... sleep on the floor... hug our favorite stuffed animal extra tight.

Daylight chases the monster away, of course. Works every time. Monsters of the imagination hate daylight.

The same goes for our irrational fears as adults. If we shed some light on our unfounded worries, they disappear. I don't like to fly, for example, and recently I found myself worrying about a round-trip flight to London. What happens if the plane runs into problems in the middle of the flight over the Atlantic Ocean? How will I handle the five-hour change in time zones? Should I pack more than one suitcase for the 10-day trip? The travel monsters under my bed were keeping me awake at night.

So, I did what we did as children—I literally shed some light on my imaginary fears. I sat at my desk, turned on my table lamp, took out a piece of paper, and listed all my fears on the left side of the page. Then I jotted down remedies on the right side.

Within 10 minutes, all my imaginary fears on the left side of the paper were erased by the realities on the right: One, statistically speaking, I'm more likely to die in a car accident on the way to the airport than in an airplane crash; two, I slept sitting up for two months after my hip surgery, so I can sleep on an overnight flight to London; three, last time I checked, hotels offered laundry service, so there's no need for more than one suitcase.

And finally, I put my imaginary struggles in perspective— how many people would happily change places with me and undertake my struggles for the opportunity to travel to London and Paris for 10 days? The answer—millions.

ROUND 2

Struggles Bring Out the Best in Us

The world breaks everyone, and afterward, many are strong in the broken places.

—Ernest Hemingway

If the author William Frost was bold enough to title his nonfiction book *The Greatest Game Ever Played*, it had better be one heck of a story with lots of drama and surprises and a happy ending to boot.

Well, this true-to-life story about a winner of a golf tournament that happened a century ago reads like a fairy tale; the unlikely champion of the 1913 U.S. Open was a 20-year-old self-taught amateur named Francis Ouimet (pronounced "we-met"), who owed his success to the struggles that shaped and sharpened him, and, in the end, gave him an advantage over the seasoned professionals he competed against.

Here is his story: Francis grew up in a small house near The Country Club, an upscale private club outside Boston in

Brookline, Massachusetts, where his father Arthur, worked as a gardener. Arthur thought golf was the frivolous pastime of the privileged class and discouraged his son from playing the game, shouting, "This game makes a mockery of everything I work for." The father insisted his son quit school at 13 and find a job, which Francis did.

But he didn't give up golf.

Young Francis became a caddie earning 28 cents per round. He scoured the rough of The Country Club for lost golf balls, and when cold, wet weather chased the members inside, Francis sneaked onto the course and practiced by imitating the swings of the best players he caddied for. Evenings after work he would practice short shots out of the deep grass or bare patches of ground in the untended field behind his house. On his rare days off, Francis would take three connecting streetcars to the only public course in Boston and play from sunrise to nightfall. But his determination paid off. In the spring of 1913, he won the Massachusetts Amateur Championship, giving him the credentials to qualify as one of the handful of amateurs invited to participate in the U.S. Open, held at The Country Club, the course Francis had traipsed hundreds of times as a caddie.

Struggles Mimic U.S. Open Conditions

Francis was honored just to receive an invitation to play as an amateur in the Open, figuring he had no chance against 145 professionals from five countries, including 1912 British Open champ Ted Ray, along with Francis's idol, the great Harry Vardon, winner of six British Opens and 62 tournaments in his career.

To further increase his long odds, Francis selected Eddie Lowery as his caddie. Just 10 years old and four feet tall, young Eddie had skipped school to attend the tournament. "I've seen you play plenty of times," Eddie said. "I can help you out there." Francis believed him, and they formed a lifelong friendship forged over four days. The final day of the 72-hole tournament was played in the pouring rain, which to Francis was golf weather.

After 72 holes, three men were tied for the lead—two seasoned pros, Ted Ray and Harry Vardon; and one 20-year-old amateur from across the street, Francis Ouimet. All three men would meet on a cold, rainy Saturday for an 18-hole playoff. A *London Times* sports report characterized the playoff as "one David against two Goliaths."

Francis Ouimet, the 20th century David, felled not one but two giants—and it wasn't even close. After 12 holes, Francis led by two strokes. By the end of the playoff, he had crushed Vardon by five strokes and Ray by six.

No Struggles, No Growth

Let's get real here—the daily struggles Francis faced to practice golf, coupled with a domineering, disapproving father, would prompt most youngsters to quit the game, no matter how much they professed to love the sport. But ironically, the struggles Francis faced—pitching and chipping from deep grass and bare ground... playing in the rain and twilight... walking 54 holes in a single day while carrying 20 pounds of equipment—ended up being the perfect preparation for the conditions he would face as a 20-year-old in the 1913 U.S. Open.

The struggles that would chase most people out of the sport just strengthened Francis's will and sharpened his game. Without the struggles, it's doubtful he would have developed the stamina to play 54 holes in two days. Or the ability to hit great shots from bad lies. Or the composure to play unaffected by cold weather and driving rain.

Francis Ouimet's struggles were a blessing in disguise, shaping him into a champion golfer and, more importantly, a champion person who would go on to found the Francis Ouimet Scholarship Fund, which has awarded more than $25 million in college tuition to underprivileged caddies.

Brave New World vs. The Old Man and the Sea

To fully understand and appreciate the necessity of struggles for a life well lived, just compare the plots and main characters in two classic novels, *Brave New World* by Aldous Huxley and *The Old Man and the Sea* by Ernest Hemingway. The books offer totally opposite views about the value of struggling.

In his satirical novel *Brave New World,* Huxley describes a futuristic Utopian world without struggles, a world where an all-powerful government controls the population by promoting pleasure while eliminating pain. To eliminate the pains that accompany struggles, the government outlaws the institutions that create emotional attachments in our lives, such as marriage and parenthood.

The result? No attachments means no feelings... no families... no stress... no problems. When struggles present themselves, the government offers free soma, the perfect pleasure drug that enables the upper-class citizens to live struggle-free, superficially comfortable in the moment until they pass peacefully away on 'soma-holiday' on their 60th birthday. Yes, citizens are superficially comfortable in their struggle-free existence, but the consequences of a state-controlled, pleasure-infused society in Huxley's *Brave New World* are a loss of dignity, morals, values, and emotions—in short, a loss of humanity.

Contrast Huxley's struggle-free world to the daily struggles of Santiago, the poor Cuban fisherman in Ernest Hemingway's *The Old Man and the Sea.* Santiago lives in a one-room hut with a dirt floor, surviving on fishing and handouts from the local grocer. He's poor in worldly terms, but he's rich in character, conducting his life with honor, integrity, and courage.

After a long stretch without so much as a bite, Santiago rows further into the Gulf of Mexico than ever before and hooks a giant marlin that takes him two days to land. Exhausted and bleeding, Santiago lashes the marlin to the side of his boat and rows for shore. On the way in, Santiago battles sharks attacking the fleshy marlin, and by the time the old man finally rows ashore, all that's left of the trophy marlin is a worthless skeleton picked clean by the sharks.

Santiago loses the fish, but in Hemingway's eyes he's a winner in life because he faces his struggles with dignity and determination. Unlike the characters in *Brave New World*, who anesthetize their struggles with soma and overindulgence in sensual pleasures, Hemingway's old man wrestles his challenges even in the face of imminent defeat. "Man is not made for defeat," the old man observes. "A man can be destroyed but not defeated."

Living vs. Existing

Contrast the old man's determined approach to struggles to the characters in *A Brave New World*: "And if ever, by some unlucky chance, anything unpleasant should somehow happen," says a character, "why, there's always soma to give you a holiday from the facts." The soma-soaked characters in *Brave New World* take the cowardly approach to life: They don't live; they just exist until it's time to take their final soma holiday.

Santiago, on the other hand, *lives* a good and brave and meaningful life because he engages his struggles. And when the sun rises the day after he loses his giant fish, Santiago heads out to sea once again to fish and face his struggles anew.

The novel teaches us that to live means to confront and wrestle with the difficulties that life throws our way, recognizing that we will all lose ultimately because we are mortals; but to live means to face our struggles honestly and passionately in spite of that knowledge. By wrestling our struggles, we define ourselves and shape our futures.

Struggles Are Our Sculptors, We Are the Stone

While we're in the midst of struggles, we'd be hard-pressed to endorse the value of struggling.

But the truth is, struggling is a blessing in disguise.

Honest.

Years ago I read a story about a teenage girl that illustrates how struggles touch us and shape us in ways that taking the easy road can't do. Here's a true-life story of how struggling brings out strengths in us that we never knew we had.

A multimillionaire man had only one child, a very spoiled teenage daughter who was about to turn 16. For years the daughter had begged her dad for a new red Corvette for her 16th birthday. The cost of the car wasn't a big concern for the father. He had money to burn. What concerned him was the idea of his inexperienced, irresponsible child behind the wheel of a high-powered sports car.

So, whenever his daughter brought up the Corvette, the father kept hemming and hawing, refusing to commit to her one and only request for her 16th birthday present. Finally, the big day came. The daughter rushed to the garage door to see if her car was parked inside the garage. Taped to the door was a birthday card with these instructions printed on the envelope:

"DO NOT OPEN UNTIL AFTER YOU ENTER THE GARAGE."

The daughter grabbed the envelope, flung open the garage door, and switched on the light. And sure enough, there was her new red corvette. It was perfect, sparkling and gleaming… but there was one big difference between this Corvette and the ones she'd seen on car dealership floors since she was 10 years old. *The car had been stripped down and carefully taken apart, and the parts were scattered all over the garage floor!*

The girl gasped when she saw the car stripped apart, engine and all, and, with tears welling up in her eyes, she tore open the birthday envelope. She flipped open the card and was greeted with her father's hand-printed message:

"Congratulations! Here is the new Corvette you so desperately wanted. Below is the name and phone number of a master mechanic who will help you to reassemble the car. As soon as it's put back together, it's yours to keep. Happy birthday! Love, Dad."

Why Struggles Enhance Owning

Once the daughter worked her way through the predictable hysterics… and once she realized this was no joke and her father meant what he said, the girl called the mechanic, and working evenings and weekends, she began the painstaking process of putting the car back together.

Six months later, the girl backed her little red Corvette out of the driveway and guided it down the street, cautiously obeying the speed limit and making a full stop at each stop sign. Not surprisingly, from that day forth, she obeyed every traffic light and washed the car inside and out once a week, even in winter. Friends stopped asking if they could drive her car—the answer was always an abrupt "NO!"

Twenty years later, she still owned the car, which was in mint condition, and she made it clear she had no plans to ever get rid of it. For years she serviced the car herself, although in a pinch she'd allow the mechanic who helped her put it back together to perform the major services at 50,000 and 100,000 miles.

In short, because she *earned* her car, she owned her car in the truest sense of the word, and she planned to keep it until the day she died.

Lessons Learned

No one can argue that the girl didn't have to struggle to get her dream car on the road. But was the struggle worth it? Absolutely. Not only did her struggles gain her a car, they also gained her valuable character-building lessons that she could rely on for the rest of her life. Lessons like the importance of discipline and teamwork... a heightened sense of self worth that comes from setting and accomplishing goals... the value of delayed gratification... and the feeling of accomplishment that comes from hard work—to say nothing about her on-the-job training as a car mechanic. In effect, this 16-year-old "spoiled" kid received a crash course in adulthood, forcing her to make essential connections between positive actions and positive consequences.

She not only got a car.

She got a blueprint for living a happy, productive life.

"Logical consequences are the beacons of wise men," said Aldous Huxley, the author of *Brave New World*. The logical consequences of persevering in the face of struggles, like the girl in the story, is that the struggles will make us wiser, stronger, and more resilient, better able to deal with future struggles that will inevitably pop up in our lives.

ROUND 3

Why Happy People Seek Struggles in Life and Business

*Happiness does not lie in happiness
but in the achievement of it.*

—Fyodor Dostoyevsky,
Russian novelist

I want to be happy. You do, too, no doubt.

Well, according to *Psychology Today* magazine, the best way to be happy is to seek unhappiness.

Huh?

Research shows that happy people seek out activities that cause them discomfort in the short term because in the long term, those temporary painful activities, like daily morning exercises, act as springboards to higher peaks of health and happiness.

"Truly happy people seem to have an intuitive grasp that sustained happiness is not just doing only the things you like," reports Todd Kashdan, a psychologist at George Mason University. "It also requires growth and adventuring beyond the boundaries of your comfort zone."

In short, happy people seek struggles in their lives.

Why Struggles Lead to Happiness

A study of more than 10,000 people in 48 countries discovered that across religions, cultures, and countries, people rated happiness at the top of their list of pursuits in life, even ahead of getting rich or being famous.

Most people would describe happiness as a calmness or contentedness... a feeling that in the moment, we're in harmony with our world. It turns out that activities that lead us to feel stress, uncertainty, and discomfort are associated with some of the happiest moments of our lives. Parenting is a perfect example.

Why would women volunteer to suffer through months of morning sickness, swollen ankles, and weight gain culminating in hours in labor? Because those nine months of struggles result in the birth of a baby, one of the happiest moments in the lives of both men and women. And, as every parent will tell you, parenting is certainly *adventuring beyond the boundaries of your comfort zone*, to borrow psychologist Todd Kashdan's language.

Do parents sometimes feel that the struggles of parenting outweigh the joys? Yes. But would most parents say the struggles are worth it? Yes again. Why? Because the heat of struggles fueled by love is what steels the bond and forges the family, the most important group in our lives.

As a father and grandfather, I can tell you firsthand about the financial and emotional struggles of raising children in today's anything-goes world. But without hesitation I can tell you that some of my happiest moments were associated with fatherhood—reading *Curious George* books at bedtime... grilling hamburgers and hotdogs at birthday parties... cheering at volleyball games... careening down water slides at Adventure Island... snapping photos at dance recitals and school graduations. I cherish those moments and hundreds more.

Two Kinds of Struggles

As I see it, there are two basic kinds of struggles: struggles we **EMBRACE**... and struggles we **ENDURE**. Struggles we *embrace* are the ones we seek to enrich our lives or challenge ourselves, such as choosing to become a parent or training to run a marathon or starting a new business. *Embraced struggles* enhance our lives by challenging us to do more... have more... and be more by daring to dream and by overreaching the ordinary and the obvious.

Struggles we *endure*, on the other hand, are involuntary; they choose us instead of us choosing them, such as losing a parent at a young age or battling cancer. In this chapter, we'll focus on struggles we embrace, and in the next chapter, titled *And You Think You Have Struggles?*, we'll talk about struggles that some unfortunate people are enduring with dignity and determination.

What Are You Willing to Struggle For?

So, what do you want most in your life? Accolades? Awards? Money? Meaning? Purpose? Pleasure? Fame? Family? Respect? Recognition? Health? Helping others?

Pick one or pick 'em all, it doesn't matter—they all come with a struggle. As the old saying goes, *If you want to move the wheelbarrow, you have to push it.* (Sadly, today too many people want the wheelbarrow to come equipped with a motor and remote control courtesy of the government. But that's another story for another time.)

Before I tell you stories about people who embraced some monumental struggles, I'd like to take a moment to tell you a cautionary tale about a couple who wanted to take a shortcut to their dreams, in their case, riches. They went from rags to riches overnight... and then back to rags in a matter of months because they skipped the struggles that come with earning money the old-fashioned way—by working for it.

Here's their sad story of their own making:

In May of 1990, Rhoda and Alex Toth were down to their last $27.20. Alex decided to drive to the local convenience store and spend $5 on a lottery ticket. It turned out to be the winning number for $13 million. They chose to take the money in yearly payments of $670,000 for 20 years. "It was my worst day," Rhoda said in an interview with *The Tampa Tribune*.

The Toths' lived large for a while. They flew frequently to Atlantic City and Las Vegas, taking friends along for free. They gave away new cars and paid off friends' mortgages. "We took care of people we didn't even know," Rhoda said. "The more you did for people, the more they wanted." They bought a 3,000-square-foot home and installed a $100,000 swimming pool. Life was good.

And then it wasn't. The IRS said the couple owed $3 million in back taxes and filed criminal charges. The house was foreclosed on. The IRS suit stressed Alex so much that he had a heart attack and died before the couple went to trial. Rhoda pleaded guilty and was sentenced to two years in federal prison. When she got out, the federal government gave her $50 in cash and a $152 bus ticket from Fort Worth to Tampa, Florida, where she rents a dilapidated mobile home. "I don't have a penny in my pocket," she says.

Today she lives on $1,084 a month from disability, from which the IRS garnishes $100. Her husband's dying wish? He asked her to buy a lottery ticket for him. She did. And she won $5. Some people are just lucky, I guess.

Just Do It

Now let's shift to a story that's the polar opposite to the Toth's. Like the Toths', Nick Woodman, CEO of GoPro, an online camera retailer, admits to being lucky, too: "I was very lucky that I had my idea when I was young," says Woodman, who was 26 when he founded the company. "I had very little overhead, and I could go live out of my Volkswagen bus while I got my company going."

A very different view of luck, isn't it? The Toths' wanted riches struggle free, and they got it. And then blew it. All Woodman wanted was an opportunity to keep his costs down while he struggled to build his business.

"People would ask me, 'Are you really doing this?' So I put a Post-it note by the side of my bed that said, 'I am doing this,' and every morning when I woke up, I'd look at that Post-it note."

After three months of waking up to his positive affirmation and getting pumped up to work (which was five feet across the room from his bed), he realized, "Hey, I'm doing this." A few months turned into 11 years and counting. Today Woodman's company is worth $1.75 billion, according to *Fortune* magazine. "Dedicating myself to actually following through was my single biggest achievement," Woodman says modestly.

He's right. Woodman sought struggles, wrestled them, and came out a winner. He not only won financially, but he won his self respect by believing in his dream and then doing what he had to do to make it come true. Because he had the wisdom to seek struggles in business, even at a young age, he's left his VW bus behind and moved into a spectacular home.

The lottery-winning Toth's, on the other hand, got shortchanged in the long run because they chose to bypass struggles and take a shortcut to their riches.

Never Too Old

Now that we've seen how a young man sought struggles in business, let's shift gears and see how some older people are seeking struggles, even at their advanced ages. The first senior is a world-famous golfer from South Africa, 77-year-old Gary Player, a winner of 164 tournaments and nine major championships during his 60-year career.

During his playing days, the South African-born Player earned the nickname "Mr. Fitness" for his vigorous aerobic and weight-lifting routines at a time when few golfers worked out with weights or exercised apart from walking golf courses. "People said that weight training was detrimental to golfers," Player says. "I was squatting 325 pounds the night before I won my first U.S. Open in 1965."

So much for conventional wisdom.

Player's first U.S. Open win occurred nearly 50 years ago, but Player is still exercising and still fit half a century later. He recently told *The Wall Street Journal* that he does 1,000 sit-ups and push-ups every morning in addition to his daily cardio routine. Did I say "fit?" Make that "ripped!" *ESPN The Magazine* selected Player to be one of the seven athletes to pose for the magazine's annual "Body Issue." The average age of the other athletes is 26, a startling 51 years younger than Player.

At 80, Japan's Yuichiro Miura is one of the few senior citizens who could claim to be more fit than Player. In the spring of 2013, Miura climbed to the peak of Mt. Everest, an amazing accomplishment considering there have only been 5,000 attempts to climb the 29,000-foot mountain over the years, with 200 climbers losing their lives on the treacherous climb. To complicate matters, Miura had surgery to repair a broken hip when he was 78 and heart surgery only four months before his climb. Miura is no stranger to the struggles of mountain climbing, having reached the summit twice before, at ages 70 and 75.

At a time when most of his contemporaries would consider 18 holes of cart golf strenuous, why would Miura, an 80-year-old coming off heart surgery, seek to risk frostbite, avalanches, and sudden 60-mile-per-hour windstorms in below-freezing temperatures for 10 days to climb up and down a mountain?

"It is to challenge my own ultimate limit," writes Miura on his website.

What Happens When People Refuse to Seek Struggles?

Struggle-free Utopias exist only in our imaginations, typically in centuries-old myths passed down for generations. One of my favorite myths is from Eastern Europe, and it's about how the first people were so lazy they nearly destroyed themselves.

According to the myth, the first people lived perfect, struggle-free lives in an abundant tropical valley. Fruits and vegetables were always ripe and grew knee high, so people could bend over and pluck them. And bread grew from trees, so people could reach up and pick it off the branches.

But without struggles, the people became lazier and lazier. They became so lazy they couldn't be bothered to reach up to pick bread off low-hanging limbs—they decided it was too much of a struggle. They set fire to the trees so that the bread fell into their hands. The fire burned up the bread trees and fruit and vegetable vines, and the people had to learn to plant and harvest fields and bake bread in order to survive.

The moral of the myth? People weren't designed to do nothing all day. We weren't meant to live like the worry-free, pleasure-seeking Alphas in *Brave New World*. We need challenges in our lives. In short, we need to seek struggles or struggles will seek us.

Don't Sleepwalk through Life

I'm all for accepting challenges. It's why people run marathons, enter Ironman triathlons, swim the English Channel, and participate in "mud runs," three-mile-plus runs over and around dozens of obstacles, culminating in a 50-yard crawl through a knee-deep mud pit.

But what is it about challenges that entice people to struggle through months of training culminating in having to endure hours, or even weeks, of strain and pain? I think the best answer comes from another super senior, 75-year-old Dustin Hoffman, star of dozens of movies since the 1960s, including *The Graduate*, *Rain Man*, and *Tootsie*. In 2012, Hoffman signed up to direct his first feature film, *The Quartet*, a sweet-tempered movie about the goings-on in a stately retirement home for musicians and singers.

When asked why he took on the arduous, stressful task of directing in his mid-70s, Hoffman replied, "The challenge in life is to try as hard as you can and then to find that in the most alive way. And not to stop until you feel it's alive, even if it falls short of what you thought it should be. That aliveness is all important."

Hoffman understands what Hemingway understood and expressed in his novels and short stories. It's what motivates a 16-year-old Australian, Jessica Watson, to sail solo around the world and an 80-year-old to climb the world's highest mountain.

To live is to struggle. So let's seek struggles and choose which mountains to climb while we still can.

ROUND 4

So, You Think You Have Struggles?

Although the world is full of suffering,
it is full also of the overcoming of it.

—Helen Keller

This will be a short chapter—necessary, but short.

It will be painful to read because it's about people who must *endure* struggles not of their own choosing.

Their struggles didn't come from bad choices. Just bad luck.

I've selected only two stories for this chapter, one about *emotional struggles* and the other about *physical struggles*. But the stories are universal because they're emblematic of the millions of people around the globe who got a bad drawing in life's lottery.

The two people you'll read about don't deserve what they must endure. It's not fair. It just is. So, they endure, day in, day out, a moment at a time.

Every Parent's Nightmare

The first story about emotional struggles is very personal to me because the woman I'm going to tell you about, Mary Jane, has been a dear friend of mine for 45 years. She was my first serious girlfriend after I graduated from college, and we've stayed in touch ever since.

First, some background on Mary Jane. When we first met, she was finishing up her nursing degree in Springfield, Illinois, where I had accepted a job teaching high school English. She was small and pretty and smart and fun, so, of course, I was instantly attracted to her. She was also a bit of a bohemian, with a restless, independent streak, which I shared. Although she was professional and dedicated to her career as a nurse anesthetist, outside work she expressed her unconventional side by restoring antique furniture, collecting quirky art, playing rock 'n' roll music from breakfast to bedtime (her favorite Beatle was, of course, John Lennon), and dressing in quasi-hippie fashion, with wide, colorful headbands and hand-beaded moccasins.

Calling her cute doesn't do her justice. She was adorable.

But we were young in all the worst ways and uninterested in settling down in our early 20s, so our short romance morphed into a lifelong friendship, and we stayed in touch through moves and marriages.

Shortly after my move to Florida in 1986, I received a call from another friend from my days in Springfield to deliver tragic news: Mary Jane's only child, her daughter, Autry, had been struck by a car driven by an illegal immigrant who ran a stop sign, explaining to the police that she didn't know what the word "stop" meant.

Autry died at the scene. She was only eight years old.

The accident happened nearly 25 years ago, but whenever Mary Jane and I talk, she invariably inserts Autry into the conversation. Mary Jane doesn't get tearful when she talks about her daughter these days. Her memories of Autry are dusty and dry now, like wildflowers pressed in the pages of a favorite tragic novel she read two decades ago.

But every day, the fresh pain of possibility is reopened to Mary Jane—*What would Autry look like today, in her mid-30s? Would she live nearby? How many grandchildren will I never see? Would she follow me into nursing or blaze her own career path?* So many lost moments… lost memories… lingering questions that are answered by silence.

During our conversations, I've noticed that since Autry's passing, Mary Jane's time references have changed. Instead of time being continuous, Mary Jane divides time into two distinct epochs, like B.C and A.D.: She prefaces her memories with "before Autry [passed]" and "after Autry [passed]," as in, "… after Autry, I had to sell our house. I kept her bedroom door closed, but just walking by it… just knowing she'd lived there, laughed there, in the same structure I was living in, well, it was a constant reminder, like a heartburn that never went away."

Mary Jane's struggles remind me of novelist William Faulkner's famous line, "The past is never dead. It's not even past."

And for Mary Jane, the past is always present. Painfully present.

Redefine Possible

The second story is about the struggles of one remarkable young Canadian, Spencer West, who was born with a genetic condition that rendered the muscles in his legs useless. So, at age five, doctors amputated both legs below the pelvis. Spencer learned to walk on his hands, which he still does, although he occasionally uses a wheelchair to get around. Not only did Spencer have to endure the physical pain of surgery at a young age, but today, in his early 30s, Spencer endures blistered hands and bruised knuckles, the result of his challenging walks to raise money for his favorite nonprofit (more about that later).

For Spencer, enduring the physical pain is easier than having to endure the emotional pain brought on by the stares and whispers of strangers when he appears in public. "What defines me aren't just my legs, or lack of them," Spencer says with a smile. "What are my interests? My passions? What do I do for a job? What do I feel inside, in my heart? Those are the things that define Spencer West."

Spencer represents the millions of people around the world who, despite being dealt a bad hand in life, endure their daily struggles by playing their cards with dignity and courage and, in Spencer's case, boldness.

'Standing Tall'

"I was made like this for a reason, so I needed to know what to do with it," Spencer says in *Redefine Possible*, the 40-minute documentary about his life. What he did was engage in physical challenges that would inspire others to face their limitations and live their lives to their fullest potential. His first big challenge was to climb Mt. Kilimanjaro, at 20,000 feet the tallest mountain in Africa. In the summer of 2012, accompanied by his two best friends, Spencer navigated the steep, winding trails in his wheelchair and on his hands until he reached the summit in seven grueling days.

It was during that climb that Spencer discovered his purpose in life: "All along the path to the top were these piles of stones called cairns" [pronounced kerns], he told interviewer Charlie Rose. "Earlier hikers built the cairns to mark the path so that climbers won't take a wrong turn and get lost. And I thought to myself, 'I can be that cairn for people who feel lost, who feel the challenge is too big. If I can overcome it, so can you. Here's the path.'"

The hike to the summit of Kilimanjaro not only inspires people, it also raised more than half a million dollars for Spencer's support of Free the Children, which builds schools and provides sanitation and clean water to impoverished villages in 45 countries, freeing children and their families from the cycle of poverty.

To Spencer's credit, he's not only *enduring* monumental struggles, he's also *embracing* struggles that empower his purpose in life while helping others wrestle the bears in their lives. Spencer West may only be a half a person in height, but he's equivalent to two or three people in heart, which is why *Standing Tall: My Journey* is the perfect title for Spencer's bestselling autobiography.

Endure with the End in Sight

We all have to endure struggles from time to time, you included. But unlike Spencer and Mary Jane, in most cases, with a proper plan of action, your struggles can be reduced or eliminated.

For example, I tolerated a painful arthritic hip for two years until the pain got so bad I didn't just limp, I lurched from one room to another. I was faced with a choice—a wheelchair or hip replacement surgery. I chose surgery. Ten months after my operation, I was playing tennis pain free. The things I struggled with for two years—a painful right hip and difficulty walking— have ended, gone, to return no more (except my left hip is starting to stiffen and ache a bit, but that's another struggle for another day).

But my physical struggles are like a hangnail compared to my wife's. In 2010, Carol was diagnosed with stage 3 uterine

31

cancer. She had to endure three months of chemo and radiation, only to have the cancer reappear in the winter of 2012. Which meant more chemo and radiation. Yes, she had to endure treatments for months at a time, but she endured the all-day chemo drips and once-a-day radiation treatments knowing that the end result, living cancer-free, was well worth the temporary struggles.

Stay on the Path

I know you're having your struggles, too. We all do. We get no free passes in this life. You may be struggling with your health... your weight... your business... your finances... your kids... your spouse. I know these struggles are stressful, painful, and seemingly never-ending. But please recognize that most struggles—most, mind you, but not all— can be managed, can be overcome. You just have to endure with the end in sight, and those struggles will weaken or lessen or even disappear, only to be replaced by a different set of struggles.

Think of it this way—if a person with only half a body can wrestle a giant bear and win, just think how much easier it is for you, with a full body, to wrestle your struggles into submission.

So, start your climb, and when you lose your way, use Spencer West's story as a cairn. Then get back on the path to redefining possibility in your life—today.

ROUND 5

Black Swans and Berserk Bears

*Worry less about embarrassment
than missing an opportunity.*

—Nassim Taleb,
"The Black Swan"

What do the atomic bomb, Elvis Presley, the Arab Spring, and the Internet have in common?

They're all Black Swans. Come again?

The Black Swan theory is a term coined by Nassim Taleb in his bestselling book to describe rare, unpredictable events that have such a massive impact that they reshape our world.

First, a quick language lesson on the term "black swan": Four centuries ago, "rare as a black swan" was a popular expression in England, often used to describe events that were, from a statistical standpoint, nearly impossible, because in Europe, all swans were white. In the first 2,000 years of European history, there was never a single sighting of a black swan, irrefutable evidence that all swans were white.

Or so they thought.

Then in 1693, a Dutch explorer sailing off the coast of southwestern Australia sighted black swans. As a result, the Euro-centric theory that all swans were white was disproved, immediately negating centuries of "scientific" observation and evidence.

The Making of a Metaphor

Thus, the Black Swan becomes an apt metaphor for our inability to make accurate predictions based on observations and experience. According to Taleb, the unpredictable... the shocker... the serendipitous—in a word, luck, either good or bad—has more impact on history, both global and personal, than predictions based on past outcomes. Taleb argues that all scientific breakthroughs, life-altering inventions, historical shifts, and artistic accomplishments are Black Swans—they're so improbable and so powerful and far-reaching that no one could have seen them coming or predicted their impact.

He's right—the highly improbable can be hugely impactful.

Who could have predicted in 1955, for example, that a 20-year-old guitar-strumming singer from Tupelo, Mississippi, would forever change pop music around the globe? But that's what the Black Swan we now know as Elvis Presley did. He introduced rock 'n' roll to middle class America, and within months—first America, and then the world, got "All Shook Up" (pardon the pun) by a new kind of music featuring a singer, a couple guitars, and a drum set, the standard equipment for the thousands of bands that followed in Elvis' footsteps.

Black Swans originated from the most unlikely people and places—the airplane from the Wright Brothers in their bicycle repair shop in Dayton, Ohio... the Model T Ford from a self-taught former farm boy tinkering in a small workshop behind his house in Detroit... the personal computer from two nerds named Steve in a one-car garage in Cupertino, California.

Unpredictable and life altering—that's the one-two punch of Black Swans.

Personal Black Swans

On a personal level, Black Swans are unpredictable events that come out of nowhere and shock us, throw our plans into disarray, and send us on a path we never anticipated. In the comically wise words of Yogi Berra, "Never make predictions. There's no future in it."

"Look to your own personal life," writes Taleb, "to your choice of profession, say, or meeting your mate... the betrayals you faced, your sudden enrichment or impoverishment. How often did these things occur according to plan?" To answer Taleb's question, my life is riddled with Black Swans. In truth, none of the major milestones in my life resulted from planning, including my career, my wife, and my dearest friends. All of them seemed to tumble into my life accidentally and, fortunately for me, have worked out wonderfully.

Black Swans can be either positive or negative (I've had my share of those, too) and, as a brain-teasing twist, sometimes negative events can turn positive and positive events can turn negative. For example, my getting fired from a technical writing job at Verizon in 1988 changed the course of my life for the better... and forever. After my firing, I started writing, first newsletters, then sales and training materials for a marketing company, and eventually books, which led to my writing or co-authoring 25 books that have sold many millions of copies during my 20-plus-year career and owning my own publishing company.

All thanks to a personal Black Swan back in 1988. If I knew the address of the guy who fired me, I'd send him a Christmas card and a box of chocolates every year.

Preparing for Negative Black Swans

If, by definition, Black Swans are unpredictable, how can we protect ourselves from negative ones? Simple—first, identify the most valuable assets in your life, both *tangible*, such as your home; and *relational*, your spouse and family members. Second, identify the worst thing that could happen, such as a fire in your home or a catastrophic illness to a loved one. Then put instruments in place to protect against those worst-case scenarios.

That's why most people buy homeowners' and medical insurance, to protect themselves against Black Swans. I said "most people"—but, unfortunately, not all people. In the U.S., nearly 20% of people under age 65 don't have medical insurance. Little wonder, then, that 60% of bankruptcies in the U.S. result from unpaid medical bills.

Look, I know insurance is expensive. And yes, like you, I hate writing those monthly checks for services I hope I never have to use. My homeowners' insurance has cost me $2,000 a year for 25 years, and I've never filed a single claim. That's $50,000 for something I've never used. If I had invested that money over the same time period, I'd have $500,000 in an investment account, which is more than my home is worth.

But I religiously make those payments anyway. And so should you, because there could be a Black Swan just waiting for you to have a lapse in judgment. The people living along the coast of New Jersey when Hurricane Sandy hit in 2012 who had paid their yearly flood insurance premiums are thinking they made a really smart decision. What about the ones who saved a few hundred bucks a year by skipping flood insurance?

They got hammered, losing, perhaps, hundreds of thousands of dollars.

Ask yourself this question: Would I prefer to lose a few hundred dollars (the average annual premium for flood insurance along the New Jersey coast is $500) most years when no major hurricanes come ashore?... Or would I prefer to lose a *few hundred thousand dollars* in the unlikely event a Category 4 hurricane packing winds over 130 miles an hour hits my home?

That's a no-brainer, right? Not for the vast majority of residents in the flood-prone New Jersey coastline. Astonishingly, on the eve of Hurricane Sandy, *only 14% of homeowners along the New Jersey coast had flood insurance*. That's just opening the window and inviting a Black Swan to fly in and roost.

Keep an Axe in the Attic

At first glance, it sounds absurd to keep an axe in the attic, doesn't it? What goofy kind of advice is that? Well, in flood-prone areas like New Orleans, it's advice that can save the lives of you and your loved ones.

Because New Orleans is so vulnerable to hurricanes, "Keep an axe in the attic" is an honored axiom among homeowners. When a major storm hits and the water rises, homeowners who haven't evacuated climb to the attic to escape the rising waters. But in rare cases when the water rises high enough to be above the eaves—say, 10 feet... or 15 feet... or even 20 feet—people in the attic will drown unless they have an axe so they can chop a hole in the roof and climb to safety.

In most years, axes in attics sit and collect dust and rust. You might feel foolish for storing one up there. But in late August of 2005, Katrina's 22-foot storm surge flooded 80% of the city, and if you were trapped in the lowest-lying neighborhoods, you'd have given everything you owned, and more, to have a rusty, dusty axe in your attic.

Well, to prevent negative Black Swans from devastating our lives, we need to expand the axes in the attic advice to all the areas of our lives—not just our homes, but also our fitness, our families, and our finances. Here are a few *axe in the attic questions* that, for your own sake, I hope you answer in the affirmative:

Fitness:

Measure your waistline. When you double it, is the total less than your height in inches? (If you are six-feet tall, your height is 72 inches. Therefore, your waist should not exceed 36 inches.) If it's larger than 36 inches, you have significantly increased your odds of type 2 diabetes, heart attack, or stroke.

Do you walk or exercise at least 20 minutes a day, five days a week?

Do 90% of your meals consist mainly of fish, fruits, and vegetables?

Is your body mass index (BMI) 25 or under?

Is your blood pressure 120/80 or lower and your resting pulse less than 65 beats per minute?

Family Safety:

Do you and your children wear helmets when biking?

Does everyone secure their seatbelt before putting the car in gear?

Do you have working smoke detectors in your home?

Do you have a fire extinguisher in the kitchen?

Do you practice a fire escape plan once a year?

Do you have your dryer vent hose cleaned regularly? (50% of home fires are started by dryer lint.)

Finances:

Do you have six months of savings in an emergency account?

Do you own more *appreciating assets* (home, retirement accounts) than *depreciating assets* (cars, appliances, TV, furniture, etc.)?

Do you have a fallback source of income if you lose your job?

Are you saving at least 10% (preferably 20%) of your gross monthly income for retirement?

For every question you answered with a "yes," you get an extra axe in the attic, which you will be thankful for when a Black Swan, such as Hurricane Katrina, floods the attic of your life.

Mental Preparation Prevents a Mauling

To extend the axe in the attic metaphor, the most essential place to keep an axe is in your mental attic. Just as mental preparation is the key to winning in sports, it's also the key to withstanding Black Swans.

When Toby Burke, a wildlife biologist in Alaska, went bird watching with his wife and three children, the last thing he wanted to encounter was a berserk bear. But because he and his family live in bear country, he knew it could happen.

And, boy, did it happen.

With the temperature below freezing, Burke and his family were bundled up in layers for their adventure. As they walked along a river beach, they spotted a bear in the distance, not an uncommon occurrence in Kenai National Wildlife Refuge.

What was uncommon this time was this bear's intentions.

"The bear is coming toward us!" yelled Grace Burke, the 11-year-old daughter. The family raised their arms and made loud noises, hoping to scare the bear off. It didn't work. Less than 100 yards away, the bear charged the family.

"Get behind me!" Toby Burke yelled to his wife. Laura Burke, with her 7-month-old baby on her back, pulled her two other children behind her husband. Burke grabbed the only thing he could use as a weapon, a six-foot-long tripod with a scope attached. When the bear reared to attack, Burke held the tripod like a spear and shoved the scope sideways into the bear's mouth. The bear bit off the scope, leaving a pointed metal tip on the tripod, which Burke used to jab at the bear's face.

The bear knocked the tripod aside with a paw and lunged open-mouthed at Burke. Instinctively, he stuck is right forearm in the bear's mouth while pummeling its face with his left fist.

"I definitely felt a crushing sensation when it chomped down on my arm," he said. "But because I had heavy layers under my jacket, my arm was just really bruised up." Unable to overpower Burke, who firmly stood his ground, the bear dropped onto all fours and ambled back into the trees. Shortly afterward, two Alaskan Wildlife Troopers who arrived at the scene shot and killed the berserk bear when it charged them as they walked along the tree line.

Burke contends what saved him and his family was standing firm, instead of running, and their mental preparation: "We weren't terrified only because we knew it's a reality when you live up here," he told ABC News. "We knew this day might come. Mentally, we were prepared for that."

Final Thoughts about Bears and Black Swans

What about you?... Are you mentally prepared to wrestle the metaphorical bears attacking you and your family?

Like the Burke family, we all live in bear country, because, as I've pointed out, to live is to struggle; and as Nassim Taleb points out, highly improbable, yet highly impactful events will inevitably slam into our lives, often when we least expect it.

To survive those attacks, we must be mentally prepared to wrestle a berserk bear from time to time, for in bear country, it's not a matter of *if*, but *when*, we will get charged. And since bear and Black Swan attacks are unanticipated and unannounced, we have to be alert... nimble... and ready to rumble, don't we?

Yes, the bear will win its share of battles, as we will learn in the next chapter.

But the mentally strongest will win the war. Make sure that's you.

ROUND 6

The Bear Will Win
Its Share

Being president is like a mule in a hailstorm.
Sometimes you just have to stand there and take it.

—Lyndon B. Johnson,
36th U.S. president

If you've ever watched the NCAA basketball finals—
"March Madness," as it's commonly called—you've likely seen
the 10-second clip of the 1983 final, when the winning coach,
Jim Valvano, sprints onto the court, arms spread wide, looking
for one of his players to hug.

His North Carolina State team had just defeated Houston
and their "phi slama jama" stars in one of the biggest upsets in
the history of college athletics. Some sports fans might mistake
this as Valvano's finest moment.

But they would be wrong.

His finest moment came 10 years later at the ESPY Awards, when he delivered his moving "Don't Give Up, Don't Ever Give Up" speech. Prior to the speech, Valvano had been battling cancer for nearly a year and would pass a mere eight weeks later.

He was only 47 years old.

Words to Live By

At the end of his speech, Valvano thrust his right arm into the air and shouted the words that have been quoted in print thousands of times and replayed on YouTube more than a million: *"Cancer can take away all my physical abilities. But it cannot touch my mind. It cannot touch my heart. And it cannot touch my soul. Those three things are going to carry on forever."*

Our minds… our hearts… our souls—those three things are what gives us the strength and the courage to beat the bear.

In this chapter, you're going to hear about two teenage girls who lived Valvano's advice to never give up, no matter what the circumstances, no matter what the odds.

One cheated death.

One succumbed to death.

But in the end, both of these brave young women wrestled the bear… and won.

The first story is about a Pakistani schoolgirl, Malala Yousafzai, who celebrated her 16th birthday by giving a speech to 1,000 young leaders from more than 100 countries at the United Nations' first Youth Assembly. For Malala, it was more than an honor to address the group—it was a miracle.

The Child the Taliban Could Not Silence

Five months prior to her speech, the Taliban tried to silence Malala permanently when an assassin stopped her school bus and, just a few feet away, fired a bullet into the left side of her forehead. For several days Malala struggled for her life in a Pakistani military hospital, where part of her skull was removed to allow her brain to swell.

Once she was stable enough to travel, she was airlifted to England for emergency care. Five months and many surgeries later, with a metal plate imbedded in her skull, Malala was pursuing the passion that motivated the Taliban to attempt to silence her.

Her "crime"? Malala wanted an education.

The Taliban insists that the education of girls end at age eight and that children can be executed if they violate the Taliban's interpretation of Sharia Law. When the Taliban took over Malala's hometown in the Swat Valley, they closed hundreds of girls' schools sprinkled throughout the mountainous region, burning many to the ground.

Malala first started blogging at age 11 about the Taliban takeover of her hometown, and when her school was closed, she wrote, "They cannot stop me. I will get my education, if it is in home, school, or any place." Her defiance drew the attention of Taliban leaders, who ordered her execution. When the government regained control of the region, Malala returned to class, and in conversations and in her increasingly popular blogs broadcast in England on the BBC, she remained a relentless advocate for girls' right to education.

Declaring that Malala was a "symbol of infidels and obscenity," the Taliban ordered her execution. Since the shooting, Malala has become a symbol, all right—an international symbol representing the right of every girl and boy around the globe to receive an education.

Wearing a white shawl that once belonged to Benazir Bhutto, Pakistan's first female prime minister, who was assassinated in 2007, Malala told the U.N. audience, "Let us pick up our books and our pens. They are our most powerful weapons. One child, one teacher, one book, and one pen can change the world. Education is the only solution. Education first."

Rights, Not Revenge

In her speech, Malala made it clear she was not interested in retribution, only rights. She said during her healing she learned "to be peaceful and love everyone," citing the words and legacies of global advocates of nonviolence, including Mohandas Gandhi, Martin Luther King, and Nelson Mandela. She insisted that she was just one of thousands of victims of the Taliban:

"They thought bullets would silence us," she said. "But they failed. The terrorists thought they would change our aims and stop our ambitions, but nothing changed in my life but this: Weakness, fear, and hopelessness died. Strength, power, and courage were born."

For now Malala remains in England, attending a private girls' school in her school uniform, a badge of honor considering that only a few months earlier in her hometown, a uniform would have made Malala a target. But today, wearing the kelly green and navy blue of Birmingham's Edgbaston High School for Girls makes her proud, she told *Time* magazine, "… because it proves that I am a student and that I am living my life and learning. I want all girls in the world to have this basic opportunity."

If there were more Malalas and fewer Taliban in the world, her wishes could come true in her lifetime.

Bald Is Beautiful

Unlike Malala's story, my second story ends on a sad note. But Talia Joy Castellano's effervescent spirit and positive postings on Facebook and YouTube have inspired millions. Here is her heart-wrenching story:

At age seven, Talia was first diagnosed with a rare and aggressive cancer. Her cancer went into remission for a while but returned several years later, and Talia lost her hair during chemotherapy treatments. Rather than wear a wig, 13-year-old Talia started playing with makeup to compensate for her baldness. She broadcast here lessons online, calling herself a "professional YouTube makeup guru," with the slogan "Makeup Is My Wig."

The videos of a bald, big-eyed teenager with a bubbly personality and the demeanor of a professional broadcaster were instant hits with viewers. Within months Talia had 750,000 followers, and her most popular tutorial garnered more than 8 million views. To date her YouTube channel, 'TaliaJoy18,' has had 40 million views—and it continues to grow.

When an interviewer asked Talia how she remained so positive, she responded, "When people ask me that, I'm, like, what do you want me to do, be depressed?" Then, imitating the animated character Dory in the Disney hit *Finding Nemo*, she giggled, "A little fishy named Dory told me, 'Just keep swimming, just keep swimming.'"

Talia's List Completed by Fans

On July 16, 2013, Talia's seven-year battle with cancer ended. But before she passed, the ever-upbeat Talia composed a "bucket list" of the things she wanted to accomplish before she died. She listed 74 items—some serious, some silly, as expected from a 13-year-old with a lively imagination and a love of life.

Here is a random sampling of a dozen items on her bucket list:

Things I Want to Do Before I Die

By Talia Joy Castellano

Go hang gliding

Meet a baby monkey

Leave handprints in wet cement

Jump in a pool of Jell-o

Drink from a coconut

Sing around a campfire

Stay in a cabin

Go whale watching

Give flowers to strangers

Send a message in a bottle

Cover a car with Post-it notes

Write a letter to my crush

As I said, this is a partial list (to view the entire list, Google "Talia's bucket list"). To commemorate Talia's life, which ended before she could complete her list, Talia's official Facebook page, *Angels for Talia*, encourages visitors to upload a photo of themselves completing one of Talia's wishes. Check out Talia's Facebook page—you'll see photo after photo of people drinking from coconuts… cuddling baby monkeys… and covering cars in Post-it notes.

Wouldn't it have been something if Talia and Jim Valvano had met in this lifetime? Talk about energy! Talk about positive sparks flying! But Talia didn't have to meet Valvano in person, for she lived his words until her last breath: "Cancer can take away all my physical abilities. But it cannot touch my mind.

It cannot touch my heart. And it cannot touch my soul. Those three things are going to carry on forever."

Talia's legacy is being carried on forever, literally, by people who have watched her videos... heard her story... and have accepted the challenge to complete the items on her bucket list, the ones she never had the time to do.

Dreams Do Not Die

Thousands of fans and admirers, from New Zealand to New York... from Tulsa to Tokyo... from Malaysia to Mexico are posting photos on Talia's page, proving that dreams never die—they're just handed down from one dreamer to the next.

And her two biggest dreams—to start a clothing line and a makeup line— continue to live on as well. Talia's design partner, cancer-survivor Urbana Chappa, flew to Orlando in April and the two met in Talia's hospital room and worked on sketches and ideas for the line. The designer and Talia both agreed not to use her name on the label, so Talia came up with the brand name that represents her indomitable spirit and sassy style.

The name of Talia's label? *That Bald Chick.* Now, that's sassy!

Talia's death reminds me—reminds all of us, for that matter—that death doesn't have to be the end. Death can also be a beginning, as described four centuries ago by the great English poet John Donne:

Death be not proud, though some have called thee

Mighty and dreadful, for, thou art not so...,

One short sleep past, we wake eternally,

And death shall be no more; death, thou shalt die.

ROUND 7

Bears Hibernate, but Humans Dream

The world needs dreamers and the world needs doers.
But above all, the world needs dreamers who do.

—Sarah Ban Breathnach,
newspaper columnist

"All achievement and all earthly riches have their beginning in an idea or a dream," wrote Napoleon Hill 75 years ago in his classic book, *Think and Grow Rich*. His observation about dreams is as true today as it was in 1937 when his book was first published in the midst of the Great Depression.

Just think about the things, large and small, that began with a dream—from Disneyland to donuts... from Las Vegas to lollipops... from mobile phones to Monopoly... from trains to teabags and everything in between, they all began with an idea and a dream to make that idea come to life and make a profit in the process.

That's the power of a dream.

Fascinating Facts about Hibernation

Dreaming is what separates humans from animals. That's why I say, "Bears hibernate, but humans dream." Before I talk about the power of dreams and how to make them come true, let's take a moment to talk about hibernation, a form of suspended animation when an animal's body temperature, pulse, and metabolic rate drop to conserve energy. Hibernation is commonly associated with bears, although a wide range of animals hibernate, including earthworms, snakes, snails, skunks, bees, and bats... and even some birds.

For now, let's stick with bears.

The most common bear in North America, ranging from Canada to northern Mexico, is the black bear. Males weigh 600 to 900 pounds, and they gorge in the weeks leading up to hibernation, gaining 20 to 30 pounds of fat a week to use as fuel during their six-to seven-month period of inactivity. During hibernation, they drop half their weight.

Males can sleep uninterrupted for 100 days without eating or drinking, although they may briefly leave their den to forage for food. Bears shift positions and scratch during hibernation, and most bears are light sleepers, especially a mother with newborns.

A bear's pulse drops down from 50 beats per minute to 10 beats during hibernation, and because bears somehow convert uric acid to protein, they can hibernate for months at a time without needing to lumber outside their warm dens for a bathroom break.

There you have it—the bare facts (I couldn't resist) about hibernating bears.

The Big Questions

What's scary is that some humans resemble hibernating bears, especially in the evenings and on weekends. Just like bears, most people retire to their dens and sink into cushy couches or deep-padded recliners. Lulled into a stupor by the soft light of their TV or smartphone, they enter a state of suspended animation. Their breathing slows down... their pulse slows down... they occasionally shift positions... they scratch... and they only leave their den to forage for food in the kitchen. Then it's back to the couch, back to the deep state of unconsciousness, back to being a hibernating bear.

Now for the big questions: What about you? In your spare time, are you active like a human?... productive like a human?... *dreaming like a human*? Or are you hibernating like a bear?

Dr. Norman Vincent Peale wrote in *The Power of Positive Thinking*, "I've learned through the years that anyone who thinks earnestly and sincerely—and then does something about it—goes somewhere." But before we can go somewhere, we first have to wake up from the hibernation of *where we are*, so that we can dream the dreams and do the deeds that will reveal *where we could be*.

Turn Off the e-Noise

As I see it, humans who are hibernating are only thinking about where they are, right now, in this moment. They're too groggy from participating in what I call "hi-tech hibernation"— electronic diversions that devour huge chunks of time with little lasting benefit, such as reality TV shows and video games and smartphone apps and always-on Internet non-news—to think about where they're going to be and what they have to do to get there.

As a result, in one year... five years... 10 years... 20 years, they'll be in the same place they are right now—hibernating to the glow of the latest electronic time-gobbling gadget.

This willingness for humans to narcotize themselves with e-noise reminds me of the Direct TV commercial where there's chaos all around a city. Gunmen in the streets... police cars exploding... banks being robbed... school buses on fire. The camera cuts to a masked super hero sitting on his couch watching TV while snacking on chicken wings and wiping his mouth with his cape. His super phone rings, but he's so engrossed in a movie that he ignores the phone call. The commercial ends with a deep-voiced announcer saying, "Direct TV now gives you access to 6,000 shows and movies for free. You're gonna be busy. Super busy."

The commercial is supposed to be funny, but I find it deeply disturbing. To me the message isn't about the benefits of subscribing to Direct TV. To me the commercial delivers a powerful subliminal message directed right at the pleasure-seeking part of the brain, saying that it's not just okay, *it's heroic, even, to hibernate while your world is going up in flames.* So, it follows that if hi-tech hibernation is good and heroic, then why dream when you can lobotomize yourself in front of the TV set? Why bother to dream about the future when the Soma of e-noise can drown out all your struggles NOW, this very moment? Why show initiative? Why improve yourself? Why embrace struggles that will empower you to be more... do more... have more, when all you need to be happy and fulfilled is a TV remote and a smartphone?

We're living in a Brave New World, indeed.

Think about it—do you really think it's good... it's smart... it's heroic, even, to stay "super busy" in a permanent hi-tech hibernation? That's a message for self-sabotage, if I ever heard one. Is that the message you want your subconscious to absorb? Is that the message you want your children to hear?

When I saw the commercial during the British Open golf tournament, I didn't laugh. I turned off the TV and grabbed a book.

What Is a Dream?

In a book I wrote nearly a dozen years ago, *Dream Making in a Dream-Taking World*, I defined a dream as "the mental process of pushing beyond our own and other peoples' expectations."

I think this definition has held up rather nicely over the years, as well as the following comments I wrote in the book: "Dreaming empowers us to expand our vision of what we can become... what we can do... what we can have... and what we can achieve. To paint a word picture, a dream is a mental movie that begins with WHAT IS.... And ends with WHAT COULD BE."

The only thing I would add to my description of dreaming is this: "To make your dreams come true, embrace struggles. Dreams aren't given to you—they're earned."

Talking about the power of dreams hits close to home for me because I, too, was a hibernating bear before a dream broke me out of my slumber and dramatically changed the direction of my life. Here's my story.

Dreams Can Come True

Back in the early 1980s, I was teaching high school English in Springfield, Illinois. At the age of 40, after 16 years of teaching, I was earning $22,000. And I was unhappy. I was hibernating, sleepwalking through my life. I wanted to wake up and live my life in a different direction.

It wasn't just the low pay. Money was never a big driver in my life. But I was burned out, tired of dealing with quarrelsome teenagers and tired of taking orders from higher-ups. I wanted to *be* the higher-up… I wanted to make the rules, *my rules*, and give the orders to myself. In a word, I wanted to own my own life. But that would never be possible as long as I was working for someone else, dependent upon a boss for my paychecks.

So, I began to dream.

I dreamed I could own my own life if I owned my own business.

I dreamed I could own my own life if I were financially independent.

I dreamed I could own my own life if I lived in a city I wanted to live in, instead of living in the city where my job happened to be.

I dreamed I could take my skills as an English teacher— my love of reading, my ability to write, my experience in teaching and mentoring—and transfer those skills to a career in marketing and corporate training.

I dreamed I could use my experience as an owner of income property to buy and manage apartments in my new hometown.

I dreamed of moving to Tampa, Florida, "America's Next Great City," as it was advertised in the 1980s.

So, in the fall of 1986, at the age of 40, I chased my dreams and embraced the struggles of starting a new life in a new city and operating a profitable business, something I'd never attempted before.

I packed my belongings into a U-Haul in the rain and headed 1,800 miles south to sunny Tampa, where I've lived for the last 27 years. I started five different businesses in my first three years in Florida. Three failed. I got fired twice. But the fourth business, writing and publishing personal growth and business books, flourished; and another business, my dream of owning rental property, came true, too. In 1987, I bought my first four-unit apartment building in Tampa for $75,000. Two years later I bought an eight-unit building for $190,000. I renovated them, raised rents, and then sold both properties in 2006 at the height of the market for $1.5 million, which I'm using to buy foreclosed condominiums in a luxury complex five minutes from my house.

Today I'm debt free... own a million-plus dollars' worth of property... own a well-funded retirement account... play golf and tennis three days a week, 12 months a year... and operate two profitable businesses out of my home office.

And it all started with a dream.

Still a Dreamer

I've reached a place in my life where I could retire. Most of my good buddies from my college years are retired. But not me. I'm still too busy dreaming.

I dream of buying more income properties. I dream of helping several poor but smart kids through college. I dream of taking more college classes, of reading all of Shakespeare's plays, of studying the Old and New Testament, of vacationing in London and Barcelona and a dozen great North American cities I've yet to visit—Savannah, Charleston, Philadelphia, and Williamsburg, to name a few.

And I dream of writing another book. Or two. Or 10.

"A man is not old until regrets take the place of dreams," said the legendary actor John Barrymore. Do I have regrets? Sure do. But do they outnumber my dreams? Not by a long shot. And I'm in no hurry to get old.

The Difference between a Dream and a Fantasy

There are two requirements for making dreams come true. First, the dream must be doable. It can be big, but YOU have to be able to accomplish it. That's why winning the lottery is NOT a dream. It's a fantasy. If the pot for a lottery is, say, $10 million and if every participant bought 10 one-dollar tickets, that means your odds of winning are one in a million.

Yes, someone is going to win that pot of cash. It's just not going to be you.

If, on the other hand, you want to double your income next year, well, that's doable. You may have to put in longer hours. Or be more disciplined in your work. Or add a second or third job. Or start a business you work in the evenings and weekends. But doubling your income is a dream because it's doable.

Set Goals and Get 'er Done

Dream first, then *do*—that's the key to making your dreams come true. When people learn that I write books, many of them say, "Oh, I've always thought about writing a book, too. I'd love to do that someday."

"Great!" I reply. "How about starting this evening?"

They usually laugh and say, "Well I can't do that...." And the conversation turns to a different topic. But they *can* do that. A lot of authors write in the evenings. Or early in the mornings before the rest of the family gets up. Or on weekends. If the dream is strong enough, believe me, they'll find a way.

To illustrate how to turn big dreams into small, doable goals, I'll show you the goal-setting process I use to write books. I've written a couple dozen books following this simple but doable process, so not only does it work, it's applicable to just about any endeavor.

Here's how I go about breaking a dream into daily doable tasks.

Begin with the End in Mind

Normally, it takes me about a year to write and publish a book—six months to gather material, four months to write, a month to design the cover and lay out the text, and a month to print.

I tell people that I don't write books, meaning that I don't write all 125 pages in one sitting. Nobody does that. What I do is write four hours a day, four to five days a week for four months. At the end of four months, a book magically appears.

I start by *dreaming* about a topic that I think will resonate with readers, such as people's inborn desire for independence, which led to my writing *How to Make Every Day Independence Day.* Or I may dream about why people should embrace struggles instead of avoiding them, which is the thesis of this book. Once I commit to a topic, I gather material for a few months and then begin writing. Here's the way I break my goals down:

Yearly Long-term Goal (*my dream*): Write a book this year

Six-month Goal: Read and research; make notes; collect and file content

Weekly Goal: Write a chapter a week (10 pages total, two pages a day)

Daily Goal: Write four hours a day, five days a week, 10 a.m to 3 p.m., with an hour for lunch and little chores; e.g., do a load of laundry

Making your dreams come true is a four-step process:

1. ***Dream a doable dream and write it down;*** then tape it to your laptop, bulletin board, or refrigerator

2. *Write down a start date and an end date*

3. *Break your dream down into goals*—monthly, weekly, and daily goals

4. *Day 1, get started...* Day 2, get started... Day 3, get started... etc.

All Excuses Are Equal

"The hardest part is just to start," says Debbie Fields, founder of Mrs. Fields cookies. "Too many people have a wonderful dream and just talk about it rather than do something about it."

She's right—starting is the hardest. The second hardest is *refusing to accept excuses* for not doing the daily goals. Excuses are like termites: They're usually small, they work tirelessly behind the scenes, and, unless they're exterminated, they'll devour your dream.

If anyone had excuses not to work her dream, it was Debbie Fields. When she started her business at age 21, she already had her first daughter. Four more daughters followed in quick succession. Talk about excuses *not* to work a dream. But her dream and determination were bigger than her excuses.

She opened her first store in 1977 and began franchising in 1990. Though she sold her business in the early 1990s, she remains the company spokesperson. Today Mrs. Fields Cookies has 650 retail stores in the U.S. and 80 in 11 different countries.

Did Debbie Fields have a dream? Yes, a big one.

Was it doable? Yes.

Did she allow excuses to devour her dream? No.

Did she embrace her struggles, wrestle them to the ground, and get up and move forward in her life? Obviously.

And so can you. It all begins with your dream. So, snap out of your hibernation... start dreaming... and start doing—today!

ROUND 8

Wrestling the Bear
of Business

*Seize any opportunity or anything
that looks like an opportunity.
They are rare, much rarer than you think.*

—Nassim Taleb,
"The Black Swan"

Other than being billionaires, what do Warren Buffett, Donald Trump, and Steven Jobs have in common?

Answer—from time to time, all three have struggled in business.

Let's start with the "Sage of Omaha," Warren Buffett, whom most financial experts praise as the best investor in history. Buffett has an off-the-charts IQ and has been buying stocks, bonds, and businesses for nearly 60 years, yet occasionally the bear of business still gets the upper hand.

Buffett's struggles started early in his career. When he was in his 20s and working full-time as a stockbroker, he bought a Sinclair Texaco gas station as a side business. The station lost money for a year before he sold it at a loss.

His second major setback occurred more than a half century later in 2008 and 2009, when the stock price of Buffett's investment company, Berkshire Hathaway, dropped by more than 50%, and his net worth plunged by $12 billion in 24 months.

Proves that even billionaires struggle—and when billionaires struggle, they struggle big.

Donald Down but Not Out

Anyone who has seen Donald Trump interviewed on TV quickly recognizes that Trump's ego and self-aggrandizement far exceed his wealth. But one thing "The Donald," as the New York media calls him, doesn't brag about is bankruptcy.

Why? Because companies that bear his name have filed for bankruptcy four times since the early 1990s. During one bankruptcy Trump was forced to sell his yacht and private jet to repay creditors, and banks put him on a monthly spending budget until he settled his debts.

But just when the media thinks The Donald is down for the count, he bounces back with a successful TV show… a dozen bestselling books, including one on golf… and rumored runs for president. Say what you will about Trump, he just won't go away.

"What separates the winners from the losers is how a person reacts to each new twist of fate," Trump said in *The Art of the Deal*. Love him or hate him… mock him or be moved by him, Trump understands that in business, as in life, the bear will win its share of battles. Which is okay as long as we win the war.

Trump is living proof of the old saying often attributed to Vince Lombardi: "You don't lose when you get knocked down. You lose when you don't get back up." One thing people must grant Trump is this: When the bear knocks him down, he gets back up. Again. And again. And again.

Jobs Loses His Job

Might be hard to believe, but Steve Jobs' struggles in business, and later in life, make Donald Trump's struggles look like a stroll in Central Park. But let's begin at the beginning.

Back in 1976, when mainframe computers were the size of city blocks, Jobs and his partner, Steve Wozniak, co-founded Apple Computer. The introduction of the Apple II in 1977, with an integrated keyboard, sound, and plastic case, essentially became the prototype for the personal computer, spawning the multitrillion dollar hardware and software industries and forever changing the way people lived and worked. Jobs was the president of Apple until 1985, when he hit the lowest point of his working career—he was fired from the company he founded.

Ever the entrepreneur, Jobs started NeXT computer in 1986, but his struggles outnumbered his successes for nearly a decade. NeXT never found its footing and failed to make a profit for nine years as Jobs burned through the millions he made from selling his Apple stock.

But Jobs kept wrestling the bear of business, refusing to surrender. He acquired Pixar Animation Studios, which went on to produce the *Toy Story* trilogy and *Finding Nemo*, among others, and grossing $8 billion worldwide while garnering 27 Academy Awards.

Irony of ironies, in 1996, Apple rehired Jobs as CEO. Thanks to his indomitable spirit, Steven Jobs had come full circle.

In October, 2003, Jobs' business struggles were exacerbated by health struggles, as he was diagnosed with a rare form of pancreatic cancer. Nine months later, he had his pancreas removed, but the procedure was too late. The cancer had spread to his liver, and in 2009 he underwent a liver transplant. Jobs continued to work even as his health declined, spearheading the introduction of game-changing products, such as i-Tunes and the i-Pod, the i-Phone, and the i-Pad, and pushing Apple to record profits, making it the most valuable company in the world.

On October 8, 2001, eight years after being diagnosed with cancer, Steven Jobs passed away at his home surrounded by his wife, children, and sister. His last word, according to his sister, was "Wow!"

Wow, indeed.

Wow for Jobs' vision.

Wow for his overcoming a long string of business struggles.

And wow for his brave, determined battle with cancer.

From Dirt Floors to the Top Floor

Let's switch gears from talking about the business struggles of rich and famous Americans to the struggles of Zhang Lan, the owner of a chain of swanky restaurants across China.

Comparing Lan's struggles to the struggles of Buffett and the boys is, frankly, like comparing the NFL to Pee Wee football. During the dark years of Mao's Cultural Revolution, nine-year-old Lan and her intellectual parents were sent to a work camp for "re-education." Lan tended pigs and slept on a dirt floor. In the evenings, she watched as her mother was forced to kneel in the cafeteria while holding a sign identifying her as a traitor to the revolution.

With Mao's death, China loosened its anticapitalist restrictions, and Lan, now in her 20s, accepted an offer to live with an uncle in Toronto. Her one goal was to work and save $20,000 and then return to China to start a business. "I never took a single day off while in Canada. I even worked weekends and holidays, to be paid double, and I saved every dime."

After nearly a decade, she returned to Beijing with her $20,000 and financed her first restaurant. She quickly tapped into an underserved market—an upscale dining experience combining Western ambience with gourmet Chinese dishes tailored to white-collar workers. Nearly 25 years and 40 restaurants later, Lan is now worth $500 million.

Doing Nothing Is Dangerous

Lan's journey from tending pigs to tending a chain of restaurants reminds me of the parable of the eagle and the rabbit. The story goes like this: An eagle was sitting at the top of a tree doing nothing. A small rabbit saw the eagle and asked, "Can I also sit like you and do nothing?"

"Sure, why not?" answered the eagle.

So the rabbit sat on the ground below the eagle and closed its eyes to rest. All of a sudden, a fox leaped from behind the tree, grabbed the dozing rabbit, and ate it. The moral of the story? *To be sitting and doing nothing, you must be sitting very, very high up.*

When Lan was at the bottom, she refused to sit and do nothing. Instead of being immobilized by bitterness... instead of feeling sorry for herself and accepting the role assigned her... instead of blaming the government and demanding it should compensate her for a decade spent in misery, she embraced her struggles and went to work creating a better future for herself and her son, who is now CEO of their profitable and growing South Beauty chain.

Unlike the eagle, however, now that Lan is at the top, she has no plans to stop working. Embracing struggles in life and business is what fuels successful people, which is why Lan—like her American counterparts Buffett, Trump, and Jobs—has no desire to retire and "do nothing"; like most super-successful people, they understand that living, *true living*, and struggling go hand in hand.

Father Loses Livelihood

I'll close this chapter with another story about embracing struggles in life and business, but this story, unlike the others, doesn't have a happy ending—at least not yet. But given Douglas Hall's attitude and work ethic, I predict he'll be back on his feet and his business will be back in the green in no time. Here's his heart-wrenching first reported in *The Tampa Tribune*:

In 2012, 34-year-old Hall changed careers, leaving his job as an air conditioner repairman to start his own lawn maintenance service, which allowed him to set his own hours so he could raise his three children under the age of six, including a son with autism. Hall's wife abandoned the family years ago, so it was up to Hall to wrestle the bear alone. He and the children moved in with his grandmother, and his business was picking up, so the future looked brighter. At least for a while.

But then, in the fall of 2013, thieves stole Hall's trailer loaded with his lawn service equipment. They stole more than lawnmowers, though. They stole Douglas Hall's livelihood.

"I was doing pretty good," he said. "And then this happened."

Hall had parked his Jeep and trailer against a privacy fence next to his house. The thieves broke the steering column of the Jeep, shifted it into neutral, and pushed it back enough to remove the trailer from its hitch, pull it to the street, and hitch it to the thieves' vehicle. Hall estimates it would cost $8,000 to replace the riding mower, lawn tools, and trailer. In the meantime, Hall is working for a friend who owns another lawn service. He's not making as much money as before, but for now, it keeps food on the table and hope in his heart. He says he'll just keep working, keep doing whatever it takes until the can save enough to start his own lawn service again.

"I plan to just find work wherever I can find it," Hall said, "until I can buy new equipment, buy a new trailer, and start from scratch."

So many times when I read stories like Hall's, the victim says something like, "I lost everything. I don't know what I'm going to do." To Hall's credit, he knew what he was going to do—he was going to work. He was going to embrace his struggles and build back his business and his life.

Blessings for the Hall Family

When you think about it, that's the only viable option, isn't it—to dry your tears, make a plan, and then get to work making it happen?

Well, I'm happy to report that my prediction that Douglas Hall would soon be back in business came true... and, amazingly, it only took a week for Hall to get his business going again, thanks to his determination and the help of a dozen or so people who read about Hall and came to his aid. A follow-up article in the *Tribune* reported that Hall received gifts of a trailer and lawn service equipment, plus gift cards and thousands of dollars in checks, which he plans to use to buy insurance on his equipment.

Hall's happy ending is the perfect example of what can happen when people embrace struggles, rather than avoid them. I think strangers came to his aid not so much because he was a victim of a theft, but because of the positive way he responded to adversity. No whining. No blaming. No begging.

Nope—all Hall wanted was an opportunity to get back to work and provide for his family, proving that in the end, good things happen to good people with good attitudes.

"Everything is a blessing, everything helps," Hall told the reporter. "Thank you and may God bless everybody who has helped me."

I say to Douglas Hall, "No, you're the one who deserves the thanks, Mr. Hall. Thank you for your can-do spirit... thank you for your great attitude... thank you for being a living lesson to your children. And thank you for inspiring others to embrace their struggles as nobly as you have."

You're the blessing, Mr. Hall. You're the blessing.

Hooray for Home-based Businesses

For sure, when we struggle in life and in business, most of us have more in common with Douglas Hall than we do with Zhang Lan or Warren Buffett. Like Hall, we struggle, some of us mightily, to make ends meet in an economy that has been stuck in neutral since 2007. We struggle to pay the bills. We struggle to make sure our children are safe and healthy. We struggle to save money.

I'm well acquainted with the kind of struggles Hall faced and you, too, may be facing. Been there, done that. I was two months away from being flat broke at age 43. But I kept plugging away, wrestling the bear of business, pursuing new opportunities, meeting new people, and the business I'd been working at for three years finally took off.

Did I struggle? You bet. Mightily, at times.

Was it worth it? Without question.

That's why it's so important to have a home-based business that can provide additional income, or better yet, a full-time career so that you're not dependent on someone else for a paycheck, especially a boss or CEO who makes even more money when they cut expenses by laying off loyal, hard-working employees.

I'm not alone in my thinking. *The Wall Street Journal* says, "... as we continue to dig ourselves out of the deepest recession since the Great Depression, the home is the new hotbed of entrepreneurial activity," citing that, in their words, "homepreneur businesses" are springing up in record numbers as "More individuals looking to change careers or seeking to start over after a layoff are trying to make a go of a home-based business."

Business colleges are jumping on board the entrepreneur train, also. Until the year 2000, teaching students how to start their own businesses was a sideshow in B-schools. Today there's an entrepreneurial explosion on campuses around the world. Back in the stone age of 1970, for example, only 200 colleges offered entrepreneurial education classes. According to *Fortune* magazine, today two out of every three U.S. colleges and universities, that's well over 2,000, offer classes in entrepreneurship, and they offer courses to all vocations, from social workers to farmers and even musicians.

I know—starting a business can seem pretty scary. And you will struggle at times, you can count on that. But it's well worth it considering that the upside of owning your own business is so huge—freedom... independence... calling your own shots... making your own decisions... setting your own hours... making your own way in the world.

Owning your own life by owning your own business— there's nothing that compares to it. Just ask Zhang Lan. Or Donald Trump. Or Douglas Hall. Or millions of others, including myself, who have wrestled the bear of business— and won.

Struggles and the True Meaning of Success

Success is counted sweetest,
By those who ne'er succeeded.

—Emily Dickinson,
American poet

"You've been more successful than I have," my contractor Bruce said to me as he was renovating a condo I bought in foreclosure.

I was surprised by Bruce's blunt statement, and the fact that he said it with a tinge of regret in his voice made me flinch a bit and led, that evening, to my pondering the word *success*—a word that gets tossed around so frequently in all areas of our lives—in sports... in business... in education... in entertainment... in relationships, even.

Success—what is it? Who has it? How do you get it? And why's it so important? Let's start with the definition from *Webster's*: "**Success:** a favorable outcome, as in the gaining of wealth, fame, rank, etc."

According to the first part of *Webster's* definition, Bruce was right—I've gained a bit more wealth, fame, and rank than he has. But not much more. Bruce has no debt, lives in a beautiful home, and is sitting on a good bit of money in his savings and retirement accounts. If we're concentrating on just the wealth part of the definition of success, to the average person, Bruce is very successful, his net worth easily in the upper 20% of Americans.

The 'Etc.' Part Is the Most Important Part

But I'm more interested in the "etc." part of the definition of success than the "wealth, fame, rank" part. The "etc." part is what this chapter is about. And I think it will open your mind to the true meaning of success and how you can achieve it.

My favorite definition of success comes from Christopher Morley, a highly regarded American journalist, novelist, and poet writing in the decades leading up the 1950s. Here's Morley's definition of success: *There is only one success—to be able to spend your life in your way.*

Great definition—short, simple, and, I think, it rings true and covers the wide range of successes that people seek and achieve. Because Morley's definition accommodates the "etc." part of *Webster's* definition, it allows the word *success* to apply as equally to Henry David Thoreau, the introverted, intellectual pauper, as it would to Donald Trump, the self-aggrandizing billionaire.

Trump chooses to earn exorbitant amounts of money by building gilded skyscrapers and levering the Trump brand at every opportunity. He's spending his life his way—and he's doing a great job of it. So he's a success—just ask him.

Writer and philosopher Henry David Thoreau, on the other hand, chose to live alone, nearly penniless, in a one-room cottage near Walden Woods, and his explanation certainly indicates he was spending his life exactly the way he wanted:

> I went to the woods because I wished to live deliberately, to front only the essential facts of life, and see if I could not learn what it had to teach, and not, when I came to die, discover that I had not lived. I did not wish to live what was not life, living is so dear; I wanted to live deep and suck out all the marrow of life, to live so sturdily and Spartan-like as to put to rout all that was not life, to cut a broad swath and shave close, to drive life into a corner, and reduce it to its lowest terms, and, if it proved to be mean, why then to get the whole and genuine meanness of it, and publish its meanness to the world; or if it were sublime, to know it by experience, and be able to give a true account of it in my next excursion.

These two were as different as a large diamond and a lump of coal—a rich man and a poor man... a shrewd businessman and an independent thinker... a public figure and a private person. Yet both, I would argue, were successful because they embraced their struggles so that each could spend his life in his own way.

Money: the Great Facilitator

Personally, I have no desire to live a Spartan-like life like Thoreau. His aversion to money made him dependent on the generosity of friends, who gave him land and donated materials so he could build his cabin. His precious library was made up mostly of borrowed books. Yes, Thoreau was an independent thinker, I'll grant him that much. But because he lacked money, his independence ended between his ears.

Thoreau famously said, "Money is not required to buy one necessity of the soul." Which may be true, but I give money more respect than Thoreau did, because of what it can do for us in this life. I call money the Great Facilitator, a means to an end, not the end in itself. Used wisely, money can reduce misery... improve health... increase knowledge... heighten security... strengthen families... expand education... reward labor... encourage entrepreneurship... enhance love... and foster freedom, to name a few.

So, money, the Great Facilitator, has a very valuable place in this world.

Stories about Struggles and the True Meaning of Success

For me personally, money is a facilitator of freedom, and freedom is my true meaning of success. For me, the more freedom the better—freedom from a job... freedom from a boss... freedom to choose my own projects... freedom to set my own hours... freedom to make my own decisions... freedom to work with whom I want, when I want, if I want.

Ask me to define the true meaning of success, and I'll put freedom in a class by itself. Everything else falls in line behind it. Again, that's my value system. For many people, the true meaning of success is to give back. Others think it has to do with accomplishing a personal challenge, like running a marathon or losing 50 pounds. Still others might define true success as personal growth. Or redemption. Or courage in the face of danger or even death.

We'll talk about all of those types of success in this chapter, but let's start with a feel-good story about the true success of giving back. The story begins with Bill Coccia, a retired machinist living near Tampa, Florida, who is president of The ToyMakers, a nonprofit group of retirees that builds thousands of wooden toys each year and donates them to children in hospitals and shelters. The toys also end up in emergency vehicles and police cars to calm the nerves of scared children.

From Part-time Hobby to Full-time Mission

Coccia joined the toy-making group in 1990. "I would make toys one day a week and golf the rest. Eventually, the golf went away," Coccia told *The Tampa Tribune*. Working year round, the nonprofit makes upward of 20,000 toy cars, trains, and planes each year. Not surprisingly, the parents and grandparents are as thrilled with the toys as the children.

This enterprise, like every enterprise, has its struggles. Machines break… workers get sick or pass away… volunteers don't show… and sometimes supplies of wood are hard to come by. That's why Coccia's role has expanded from toy-maker to top recruiter and lumber collector. Several times a year he makes the rounds of wood shops in the Tampa Bay area, collecting their scraps, turning grown-ups' trash into children's treasure.

Not surprisingly, Coccia soon discovered that The ToyMakers was as good for the seniors as it is for the kids, giving recent retirees to Florida a purpose in their lives and a welcoming community of like-minded folks. Which is why many of the volunteers echo Coccia's motivation for turning a part-time hobby into a full-time job:

"It's not something I have to do," says Coccia. "It's something I want to do." Don't we wish we could all say the same about our work?

A Personal Challenge Becomes a National Challenge

The next story began as a personal challenge to exercise more but soon grew, like a snowball down a hill, into a national campaign to get America back on its feet again—literally.

Harrison Milanian, a 22-year-old University of South Florida student and unemployed chef, was bored and unfulfilled. To shake himself out of the doldrums, he started walking with his two-year-old golden retriever. Soon, short walks became 20-mile daily jaunts, and a big personal challenge was born.

"The longer I walked, the better I felt," Milanian said. "My moods improved, I was doing better in school." He decided to set a giant personal goal for himself while touting the benefits of walking to an increasingly sedentary America: He would walk across the country with a sign on his back: "America on Foot."

Milanian left from Tallahassee, Florida, in May of 2013 and started walking west. He pushed a baby stroller loaded with 50 pounds of supplies for survival: snacks, a tent, five pairs of socks, five pairs of underwear, a few shirts, shorts, and six gallons of water. To add to his challenge, Milanian took no cash. His only connection to the world was a ready smile and a smartphone, on which he posted photos and a running commentary on his Facebook page.

"I took no money at all," he said. "It was a test for myself. This was like a rite of passage for me, a challenge for me. I was walking across America and I didn't bring any money to make it easier."

He averaged 30 to 40 miles a day and finished his journey in a little less than three months. Facebook was his only link to the rest of the world, but it ended up making the trip more bearable. As his Facebook views and likes expanded, so did gifts from strangers. Facebook "friends" offered him lodging, showers, free meals, water, and shoes. Good thing—he drank three to four gallons of water a day and went through five pairs of shoes.

Unforeseen Struggles and Beautiful Sunsets

"Dealing with the loneliness was the hardest part," he said. "I would be by myself a week at a time. No one to talk to." Ironically, dealing with people offered its own set of challenges: In Albuquerque, New Mexico, a half dozen members of a street gang hurled obscenities at him, demanding that he couldn't walk on "their" sidewalk.

And in Amarillo, Texas, three police cruisers and two officers on motorcycles blocked his path, demanding to know who he was and where he was headed. He smiled, held up his arm and made a two-fingered "V" for the peace sign. The police were not amused, and they handcuffed him and forced him into the back of a police car. He was released when he convinced the officers he wasn't a public nuisance—he was on a public mission.

Milanian discovered his version of the true meaning of success during his three-month cross-country trek: "Even though I had no money, it was the happiest time of my life. It was liberating to have so little while being surrounded by so much beauty. Our country is so beautiful," he said.

Yes, our country is beautiful, Harrison Milanian. And so are your spirit and attitude.

Last Story, Last Rites

This last story about the true meaning of success is the most touching and, I think, the most telling. It's about 45-year-old Susan Spencer-Wendel, a wife, mother of three, and journalist who wrote a book as she was dying of ALS, also known as Lou Gehrig's disease.

ALS kills the motor neurons that send signals to muscles. As the neurons die, the muscles atrophy, and the body slowly shuts down, one limb… one swallow… one breath at a time. As the disease progressed, Spencer-Wendel decided to write her life story. It took her three months to type it on her iPhone, one letter at a time, using just her right thumb, the only finger that worked.

Her body was dying, but not her spirit. "Swiftly, surely I'm dying," she wrote. "But I am alive today. So, it's time to stop dreaming and start doing." One thing she did was fly to New York with her 14-year-old daughter, Marina, to pick out Marina's wedding dress; both recognize that Mom will never live long enough to see her daughter walk down the aisle.

"As my beautiful daughter walks out of the dressing room in white silk, I will see her 10 years in the future, in the back room right before her wedding, giddy and crying, overwhelmed by a moment I will never share," she wrote. The parents celebrated their last Christmas together by giving money to their favorite charities and handmade scrapbooks to the children. And, of course, Susan Spencer-Wendel's gift was her book, a gift for the family and the world.

This story doesn't have a happy ending, at least not in the traditional sense. But it does illustrate the true meaning of success on several levels, the first being that the publisher HarperCollins gave her a $2 million advance for her memoir, *Until I Say Goodbye*, and Universal Studios paid her another $2 million for the movie rights to her story.

The second level of her success isn't about the money. It's about the ultimate "etc." part of success—one woman's incurable, indubitable love of life: "I am writing about accepting," she wrote. "About living with joy and dying with joy and laughing a lot in the process."

The Lasting Legacy of Love

"My muscles are dying, and they cannot return," Susan Spencer-Wendel wrote in the early pages of her memoir. "I cannot lift my arms to feed myself or hug my children. I will never again be able to move my tongue enough to clearly say 'I love you.'

She didn't need to say "I love you" because she spoke it so clearly in her actions. To my way of thinking, Spencer-Wendel embodies the ultimate true meaning of success—love of family. Love of faith. Love of friends. And love of life.

Love. Such an overused word. Such a corny word. But it's the single biggest measure of success. When we talk about the true meaning of success, we can talk about accepting challenges... about achieving freedom (my personal favorite)... about giving back and any number of other noble gestures. But in the end, the discussion will eventually turn to love, for deep inside, every human recognizes the wisdom in these words: "If we have not love, it profits us nothing."

Can't Buy Me Love

Two of the world's richest men, Warren Buffett and his business partner of 50 years, Charlie Munger, are in total agreement as to the true meaning of success, and it has little to do with making lots of money.

Here's what they had to say about achieving success at the 2013 annual convention of Berkshire Hathaway stockholders:

Buffett: *You are successful if the people who you hope to love you, do love you. Charlie and I know people who have buildings named after them, receive great honors, and nobody loves them—not even the people who give them honors.*

Munger: *You don't want to be like the motion picture executive who had so many people at his funeral, but they were there just to* *make sure he was dead. Or how about the guy who, at his funeral, the priest said, "Won't anyone stand up and say anything nice for the deceased?" and finally someone said, "Well, his brother was worse."*

Buffett: *Charlie and I talk about wouldn't it be great if we could buy love for $1 million? But the only way to be loved is to be lovable. You always get back more than you give away. If you don't give any, you won't get any. There's nobody I know who commands the love of others who doesn't feel like a success. And I can't imagine people who aren't loved feel very successful.*

Warren Buffett embodies success because he has enjoyed both parts of the definition of success—he's enjoyed the "wealth, fame, and rank" part; and he's enjoyed the "etc." part.

If I were forced to choose one part of the definition of success at the exclusion of the other, I know which one I'd choose. What about you?

ROUND 10

Grin and 'Bear' It

It's very hard to take yourself too seriously when you look at the world from outer space.

—Thomas K. Mattingly II,
Apollo 16 astronaut

*L*augh and the world laughs with you, *weep and you weep alone.*

I must have heard this old adage hundreds of times over the years, but it was only recently that I learned that it's not really an old saying—it's the opening lines of a poem called *Solitude*, by Ella Wheeler Wilcox.

Here is an abridged version that captures the essence of the poem, which was an immediate sensation when it was first published in 1883:

Laugh, and the world laughs with you;
Weep, and you weep alone.
For the sad old earth must borrow its mirth,
But has trouble enough of its own.

Rejoice, and men will seek you.
Grieve, and they turn and go.
They want full measure of all your pleasure,
But they do not need your woe.

Story behind the Poem

The inspiration for the poem came during a train trip taken by Wilcox to attend the governor's inaugural ball in Madison, Wisconsin. A young woman sitting across from Wilcox was shaking with sobs, obviously distraught. Wilcox moved next to the woman to comfort her. Wilcox learned the woman was a recent widow still grieving for her husband.

Once she arrived in Madison, Wilcox was so depressed she considered skipping the ball and remaining in her room. When she looked in the mirror, she studied her face and said a quick prayer of thanks for her own good fortune. But her thoughts soon returned to the broken-hearted widow on the train. In that moment, she recited the often-quoted opening two lines of *Solitude*: "Laugh and the world laughs with you; weep, and you weep alone."

"We are the only creatures that both laugh and weep. I think it's because we are the only creatures that see the difference between the way things are and the way they might be," said Robert Fulghum, author of the mega-bestseller, *Everything I Need to Know I Learned in Kindergarten*. In other words, when we admit to the disconnect between reality and wishful thinking, we have two choices: We can cry over our misfortune… or we can laugh at the absurdity of the situation we find ourselves in. "Those who laugh, last," says Fulghum, meaning that laughter isn't just a temporary diversion—it's a healthy coping behavior.

Finding a Way to Work

The actor Michael J. Fox, who has been battling Parkinson's disease for more than 20 years, echoes Fulghum's observation that those who laugh, last.

"Parkinson's has its advantages," Fox smiles before delivering the punch line: "Who needs an electric toothbrush when you have a vibrating hand?" He follows that with an even grimmer line in reference to the progressive nature of the disease: "I tell people that Parkinson's is a disease that keeps on taking."

"Even when Mike's symptoms are the most acute, it drives him crazy to be pitied," says actor Denis Leary, a longtime friend. "I'll walk down the hall with him, and he'll be herky-jerky, and he'll go, 'Look out, Denis, you might get an elbow in the face.'"

Truth be told, there's nothing funny about Parkinson's, an insidious disease that causes brain cells to degenerate, which triggers muscles to tremble, jerk, and become rigid, unable to respond to conscious commands. But Fox and his wife Tracy put things in perspective: "We were talking the other day about all the people we know since my diagnosis who have died of cancer or had terrible things happen to them. If you could have told those people 10 years ago that they can have their tragedy or can have what I have, they would have taken what I have. In the end, we all get our own bag of hammers."

Despite his limitations, Fox continues to work. In recent years he's guest-starred on TV series as a character with Parkinson's. "It's too difficult to hide it," he says of the disease. "As long as I play a guy with Parkinson's, I can do anything," he says. And he means what he says—in the fall of 2013, he'll star in his own comedy show on NBC about a New York anchorman whose life is shaken up by Parkinson's.

Embracing Struggles Improves Lives

Fox has testified before Congress on the need for increased funding for Parkinson's research, and in 2000, he founded the Michael J. Fox Foundation for Parkinson's Research. The purpose is to improve the lives of the millions of people worldwide living with Parkinson's. To date, the foundation has funded nearly $325 million in research and supported hundreds of scientists in more than 20 countries. "The attention Michael has brought to Parkinson's research has sparked a complete revolution," says Todd Sherer, the foundation's CEO. "Thanks to Michael, curing Parkinson's is Job 1 for some of the best minds in neuroscience."

Because Fox embraced his struggles, he has helped not only himself but also millions of others who have been, or will be, afflicted with the disease. And laughter is the key coping mechanism that allows him to remain positive.

"I try not to take myself, or my condition, too seriously," he says. "Sometimes there's no other choice but to laugh. Take clapping, for example. If I'm at events and I'm clapping," he says with a grin, "my mind will say, 'Stop clapping,' but I just keep going. Tracy says, 'You're always the last one clapping.' I swear, it's not out of appreciation—it's out of disintegration. You have to laugh at that."

Indeed, he who laughs, lasts.

Dinner with the Smileys

If your last name is Smiley, you'd better be able to tell a joke and take some teasing, which is how Dustin and Sarah Smiley and their three boys deal with struggles in their lives—with a sense of humor and a roll-with-the-punches outlook on life.

As Dustin, a 14-year Navy veteran, was about to be deployed overseas for a year-long tour in Africa, their eight-year-old son

Owen said to his father, "It will be weird not to have you at the table." Without batting an eye, Sarah said, "Then let's fill Dad's seat. We'll invite people over for dinner. We can invite someone every week if you want."

A family tradition was born on the spot.

Soon after Dustin left for Africa, Mom and sons started on their wish list for weekly dinner guests at their home in Bangor, Maine. The boys agreed to take turns inviting a new guest each week. First on the list was Susan Collins, a U.S. senator who owns a home in Bangor.

"I never expected she'd be able to accept," said Sarah, "and I encouraged the boys to invite more 'realistic' guests. But in late December I got a call from the Capitol: The senator was coming the first week in January."

In the weeks that followed, the guests kept coming: The Smileys ate with the chief of police for Bangor... a symphony conductor... an Olympic gold medal rower... a baseball historian... the local weatherman... a former governor of Maine... an illustrator of children's books... a local Star Wars enthusiast who brought along his life-size R2-D2 robot... and a zookeeper.

In the 17th week, the family dined at a local nursing home with a woman suffering from Alzheimer's disease and her husband. The evening was going nicely until the wife smeared pasta sauce on the table. Holding up a sauce-covered hand, she asked one of the boys if he'd like a bite. He politely declined. The husband explained that his wife didn't remember anything about their marriage. "The only thing she knows is that I'm her best friend," he said.

Some of the dinners turned into outings. Congressman Mike Michaud took the family to Mount Hope Cemetery to put flags on veterans' graves. A world-renowned climber helped the family scale a cliff at Acadia National Park. An artist acted as a tour guide at a museum, followed by a painting session in the back yard.

The Positive Part of Embracing Struggles

When Dustin returned from his tour of duty, he was greeted at the airport by his wife, three boys, and 60 guests from the 52 dinners hosted during his absence. That evening at dinner, the children led him to his usual place at the table. Dustin pulled out his chair. Stuck to the seat was a Post-it note. It read, "Reserved for Dad."

Everyone in the family was delighted to have Dad home, safe and sound, sitting comfortably in his reserved seat at the dinner table. But because the Smileys embraced their struggles, instead of avoiding them, Sarah and the boys were blessed with many new friends while learning scores of life lessons. "Instead of wishing away the days of Dustin's deployment, we were filling them with interesting people and role models," Sarah said. "We missed him, of course, but we seldom felt lonely."

As an added bonus, Sarah wrote a book about her year of hosting dinners for strangers, titled simply, *Dinner with the Smileys*. As time passed and the dinner guests waved their goodbyes, Sarah and the boys gradually recognized a change in the family. "Many of our remaining dinners became about recognizing our own strength," said Sarah. The newfound strength and growth that came from wrestling the bear of missing a husband and a father for 12 months became the overriding theme of her book.

Struggles Reveal Surprises

The Smileys are a perfect example of the blessings that come from embracing struggles, rather than avoiding them. The blessings of a book… the blessings of 60-plus new friends… the blessings of having a husband, and father, in the military who returned healthy and whole… the blessings of learning lessons that will last a lifetime—none of those blessings would have been if the Smileys hadn't embraced their struggles.

Having embraced their struggles, Michael J. Fox and Sarah Smiley discovered they have something in common that they never would have discovered if Fox hadn't been stricken with Parkinson's and Sarah hadn't been forced to manage the household by herself for 12 months—namely, their struggles forced them to grow closer to their spouses.

Sarah was in denial about their separation until the day Dustin knelt to say goodbye to the boys at the airport. And in the early days of the disease, Fox kept resisting his wife's help, keeping Tracy at a distance. But in the end, the disease brought them closer together.

"The more problems you solve together and the more experiences and laughs you have, the tighter you get," says Fox. Which is what embracing struggles is all about—solving problems and sharing experiences with the people that mean the most in your life.

The Right Thing to Do

Perhaps the most important lesson Sarah and her sons learned came from meeting people with problems far greater than theirs. During a Memorial Day dinner, principal Lynn Silk told about losing her son, an Army staff sergeant, in a helicopter crash. And for one dinner, the boys took a newly widowed neighbor to lunch at a downtown bakeshop. "You don't have to be alone," 10-year-old son, Ford, told her. A few weeks later, Owen missed a friend's birthday party to attend the funeral of another neighbor.

"It's the right thing to do," he told his mom.

When you ask yourself, "Why embrace struggles when it's easier to ignore them… or avoid them… or pretend they don't exist? My answer? For the same reason 10-year-old boys attend funerals and comfort widows—it's not always the easy thing to do. *But it's the right thing to do.*

So, do the right thing for you and your family—embrace your struggles, and they will deliver blessings you never anticipated.

CONCLUSION

CONCLUSION

'I Work, That's What I Do'

Life is an escalator: You can move forward.
Or backward.
But you cannot remain still.

—Patricia Russell-McCloud,
author and speaker

My friend Bruce is a bit of a medical wonder.

By all rights, he should be dead—two or three times dead.

Bruce has survived not one, but two heart attacks, and he recently discovered he has a heart murmur caused by a faulty aortic valve. If that's not enough, he's survived surgery to remove a cancerous prostate... endured six weeks of chemotherapy and two weeks of daily radiation... and undergone two more major surgeries related to his cancer.

Despite the surgeries and chemo, he thinks the cancer may be spreading to his bones. His back and shoulders ache constantly. He's lucky to get an hour of uninterrupted sleep. He has night sweats and hot flashes, common side effects after prostate surgery. And arthritis prevents him from straightening his left arm, which is especially inconvenient because he's left-handed.

Oh, and Bruce just turned 70. So, at his age and with all of his medical issues, you'd think he'd be nodding off in his wheelchair while waiting for lunch at a nursing home.

But you'd be wrong.

Can You Keep Up with This Schedule?

I only know Bruce's medical history because we've spent lots of time together since 2009, when I hired him to help renovate a condo I bought in foreclosure. Since that time, he's been my one-man renovation crew. I originally hired Bruce to do some electrical work, but I quickly discovered he could do everything I needed—electrical, plumbing, carpentry, tile work—you name it, he could do it faster and better and cheaper than 99% of the contractors in the Yellow Pages.

So, as I acquired new properties, most of which were in desperate need of a major makeover, I kept expanding Bruce's tasks and kept using him. As I write this, he's renovating my seventh condo in four years. When he's done with this condo, I'll turn him loose on my house, which is sorely in need of some upgrades.

When Bruce is rehabbing one of my condos, he works a full eight-hour day—and when I say work, I mean work. We live in Tampa, Florida, where the daytime weather hits 90 degrees and 80% humidity from June through October. And that's outside. In the shade. With a breeze.

Six of my condos are upstairs units, which means for Bruce to rewire a property, he has to crawl around in the attic for two, three hours at a time, where temperatures can hit 120 degrees in dead air. After the electrical is done, he's likely on his knees tiling floors… or on his back replacing the plumbing… or in the parking lot carrying 77-pound sheets of drywall from his van to a condo, usually up two flights of stairs. And he does this eight hours a day, four to five days a week, at 70 years old, with a bad heart.

But that's not all.

After work, two days a week Bruce plays tennis for a couple hours. And on the afternoons he isn't playing tennis, he's golfing 18 holes with his wife Dianne, or walking nine holes with me at a nearby country club. You'd think he would take Saturday off, but that's reserved for yard work—hand mowing, weeding, pruning, mulching—you know, the grunt work that has to be done, especially in Florida in the summer growing season.

Doing and Being

Now, there are two reasons people work—because they have to, or because they want to. Bruce is the latter. He has no debt. No car payment. No mortgage. And has tucked away a good bit of money in retirement accounts. And he can squeeze a nickel until the buffalo stampedes.

He can afford to be 100% retired. Don't get me wrong—he likes the money he makes as a contractor. He certainly wouldn't do what he does for free. But for Bruce, working is about more than the money. Working is about the satisfaction that comes from embracing struggles. Working is about purpose. Working is about meaning. Working is about living.

"I work, that's what I do," he said to me one afternoon on the golf course. "I can't sit still. I don't like reading, it's too passive. I like working, solving problems, improving property, making a difference. That's what I do, and I'll do it for as long as I physically can."

You see, Bruce understands the value of embracing struggles in your life. For sure, he's had to wrestle that bear of bad breaks by *enduring* struggles not of his own choosing. Cancer. A bad heart. The aches and pains and indignities of aging. But he doesn't sit in the corner and feel sorry for himself. He chooses not to wallow in self-pity—that only moves you backward on the escalator of life.

Bruce chooses to *embrace* struggles because, well, by embracing struggles, he defines himself as a doer, and to Bruce, doing and living... doing and being... are one and the same. To Hamlet's famous question about the meaning of life—"To be or not to be, that is the question"—Bruce's answer is *to be* by working, by embracing struggles that most people with his resources would avoid.

What Do You Choose to Become?

"The highest reward for man's toil is not what he gets for it, but what he becomes by it," wrote John Ruskin, the English artist and social critic.

That's why struggles exist—to help us *become*.

When we wrestle that bear by embracing struggles, rather than avoiding them, we *become* a fully engaged human being... we *become* what we were designed to become... we *become* worthy of this gift we call life.

Another great English writer, George Eliot, challenged us with this statement: "It's never too late to be who you might have been."

Conclusion: 'I Work, That's What I Do'

So, start becoming who you might have been....
Start wrestling that bear, start embracing struggles—today!

NOTES